PARENT & CHILD

Getting Through to Each Other

LAWRENCE KUTNER Ph.D.

AVON BOOKS ◆ NEW YORK

AVON BOOKS
A division of
The Hearst Corporation
1350 Avenue of the Americas
New York, New York 10019

Copyright © 1991 by Lawrence Kutner
Cover art by Anne Marsden
Published by arrangement with the author
Library of Congress Catalog Card Number: 90-40865
ISBN: 0-380-71368-3

Published in hardcover by William Morrow and Company, Inc.; for information address Permissions Department, William Morrow and Company, Inc., 1350 Avenue of the Americas, New York, New York 10019.

The William Morrow and Company edition contains the following Library of Congress Cataloging in Publication Data:

Kutner, Lawrence.
    Parent & child : getting through to each other / Lawrence Kutner.
        p.   cm.
    Includes indexes.
1. Parent and child—United States.   2. Child rearing—United States.
3. Child psychology—United States.   I. Title.   II. Title: Parent and child.
HQ755.85.K88   1981
649′.1—dc20   90-40865
                                                                              CIP

First Avon Books Trade Printing: March 1992

AVON TRADEMARK REG. U.S. PAT. OFF. AND IN OTHER COUNTRIES, MARCA REGISTRADA, HECHO EN U.S.A.

Printed in the U.S.A.

OPM   10   9   8   7   6   5   4   3   2   1

Acknowledgments

No PIECE of published writing is solely the work of the author whose name appears on the cover. Although I take responsibility (or blame) for the words in this book, I have many people to thank for their direct and indirect help with this project.

Several hundred psychologists, psychiatrists, social workers, sociologists, parents, children, and the occasional economist and accountant shared their valuable time with me during interviews for my *New York Times* column. Their contributions have been incalculable and, indeed, form the heart of what I have written.

The ~~many~~ editors at *The New York Times,* who have spent the past few years polishing my prose and whipping me into shape while I received all the credit, have helped me ~~a great deal~~ immeasurably in my growth as a writer. Although there have been many of them, five stand out. Jane Traulsen and the late Dona Guimaraes developed the idea for the "Parent & Child" column and served as its principal editors for its first two years. Stephen Drucker and Yanick Rice Lamb have edited the column since 1989. The column bears their imprint, even though their names have never appeared. Margot Slade, who recommended me for the job and who guided and emotionally supported me during my first few months, has earned my undying affection and thanks.

John R. Thompson, Ph.D., of Oberlin College, introduced me to clinical psychology nearly two decades ago and sparked my interest in understanding why people behave the ways they do. The late John Brantner, Ph.D., of the University of Minnesota, served as my graduate school adviser and was one of the few professors at the time to encourage me to combine psychology and journalism.

Thomas G. Mayer, M.D., of Minneapolis, under whose guidance I delivered my own son into the world, has provided me with continuing reassurance, support, and information about child development.

Melvin and Renée Slade acted as my surrogate parents during a very frustrating time of my life. Their unqualified and unquestioning love and support helped me learn that the need for parents does not stop at adulthood.

Sol and Roz Kutner, my cousins, reintroduced me to the meaning of a family at a time when I was becoming quite cynical about it. The joy and love they share with those who are close to them are a delight to behold and to feel.

Emily Reichert, the first editor of this book, has somehow been able to tell me to rewrite, reorganize, or throw out sections and at the same time make me feel excited about the extra work. It is a rare gift that is much appreciated.

Adrian Zackheim, who took over as the book's editor, has shown tremendous faith in me and in my work. I look forward to a long and fruitful relationship.

Al Lowman, my agent and good friend, has never flagged in his support and encouragement throughout the creation of this book. His faith in my abilities has given me the courage to try new things. His humor has buoyed me up when I feared I would sink.

The influence of my parents, Michael and Mary Kutner, is profound and unquestionable. They taught me to challenge hidden assumptions, not to believe in the trappings of power, and to have faith in myself. Their most important lessons, however, came from what they did rather than what they said. For as long as I was with them, I knew that I was wanted and I knew that I was loved. I wish I had known them longer.

My wife, Cheryl Olson, has been an inspiration. To say that I could not have done the book without her is an understatement of grand proportions, for she combined her unceasing encouragement with her excellent skills at editing and organizing. Her patience with my moodiness, as I vacillated between frustration and elation, is appreciated far more than I have ever expressed.

Finally, I must doff my hat to our son, Michael, who, I am sure, will give me a thorough critique of this book once he learns how to read.

Contents

Introduction

A Chinese restaurant I'm especially fond of recently changed the brand of chopsticks it gives to patrons. What struck me about the new chopsticks was not their shape or size, but that they come with an illustrated instruction manual. It's only three crude drawings and a few phrases of fractured English printed on a paper slipcase, but it is still a manual.

Everything from airplanes to kitchen blenders—and even chopsticks—comes with an instruction manual. Children, despite all their complexity, do not.

There are many excellent books on the market that talk about the mechanics of child development and parenting. What should you do when your two-month-old won't stop crying? When is a good time to toilet train your child? What details should you tell a five-year-old about sex?

This book is different, for it is an attempt to enter the mind of the child and to see things as a child does, without the assumptions and experiences of an adult. This is no simple task. It requires an understanding of how children communicate with themselves, other children, and adults, especially how they communicate with their parents.

From the moment they are born, children try to make sense of the world that surrounds them. Yet to adults, a child's behavior often makes no sense because those adults are viewing the world from their perspective instead of from the child's.

That difference in perspectives is not trivial. After interviewing several hundred child development researchers, clinical psychologists, child psychiatrists, parent educators, and others for my "Parent & Child" column in *The New York Times,* I noticed a very clear pattern. Almost all the parents who find child rearing very frustrating have one thing in common: They are unfamiliar with the natural history of childhood, with what types of behavior are natural and appropriate at different stages of a child's life. These parents often have unrealistic expectations for their children and for themselves. They misconstrue their children's attempts to communicate by applying an adult's perspective to a child's behaviors.

All parents do this to a certain extent, of course. We each forget what it is like to see things and, more important, to think like a child, without the knowledge, perspective, and assumptions we carry with us as adults. That is where this book fits in. Gaining a better understanding of how children's minds work at different ages will allow you to make more sense of their behaviors. With this understanding come decreased stress and increased pleasure from being a parent. It lessens the frustrations that come from expecting things that a child simply cannot do or from incorrectly interpreting a child's behavior in adult terms. It reduces the instances when, as a friend of mine succinctly put it, "All of a sudden I heard my mother's words come out of my mouth. They were the words that I swore, as a child, I would never say to my own kids."

Childhood is filled with magic. Unlike the magic of stage illusions, which lose their charm when the underlying methods are exposed, the magic of childhood becomes more compelling the more it is understood. Why does a game of peekaboo elicit giggles of delight in a one-year-old? What does it tell us when a three-year-old can sleep through noises and movements that would awaken a child a few years older? Why do college freshmen behave so strangely during their first visits home from school?

But this is not a book of theory. It is, I hope, a very practical book that offers down-to-earth ways to help your children and you based not only on the experience of parents but also on some of the cutting-edge research and clinical work in child development, education, psychiatry, and psychology being done in universities, medical centers, and schools throughout the world. Such information is often difficult for parents and even psychologists and psychiatrists to obtain and to interpret, for the nuggets of practical information may be buried among statistical tables, convoluted technical terms, and professional jargon. My task, in both my newspaper column and this book, has been to extract those nuggets of practical material and to share with you information and techniques that make as much sense in your home as in an ivory tower. Here are two examples:

How does a seven-year-old understand the death of a classmate or a relative? What types of behavior are normal? What are the signs of trouble? What can parents do to help? The work of researchers with the Harvard Child Bereavement Study and the clinical experience of Dr. Sandra S. Fox, director of the Good Grief Program at Judge Baker Children's Center in Boston, to choose two resource centers, can give parents the insights and the tools needed to handle this delicate situation.

A second example: What are the unsung benefits of arguing with your children? How can battles with a preschooler over finishing vegetables at dinner actually help prepare that child for grade school? Why do the number of fights between parents and children increase during puberty, and what does that have to do with the behavior of apes in the wild? Work by Dr. Leon Kuczynski at the University of Guelph in Ontario on how children learn negotiating skills and by Dr. Laurence Steinberg of Temple University in Philadelphia on parent-child arguments during adolescence can help put these inevitable disagreements in perspective.

Understanding more about how children's minds work will allow you to help them cope with the tasks of growing up. The recommendations of experts and results of developmental psychology research will make more sense. You will sharpen your intuition and have more fun.

This book is divided into two parts. The first section explores the nature of being a parent and communicating with children. How is the family evolving from what we grew up in when we were children? What difference does this make to children today? What are the false assumptions about being parents or being adults that we have brought with us from childhood? How does the "job description" of being a child change from year to year?

The second section examines new ways to understand children's behaviors and parent-child communication. Which approaches to discipline work best, and why? What can parents do to help children learn to be empathic? How can you help children of different ages cope with the death of a relative or friend? What can help children handle the stresses of divorce? How can you teach a child about sexual responsibility? How can you help your adolescent avoid problems with alcohol and other drugs?

Unlike most books on child development, this one does not present the analyses and advice in strict chronological order. There is no section that talks only about babies or only about toddlers. (We have, however, included an age-finder index that allows you to find references to children of a particular age-group.) Part of the wonder of childhood and the joy of raising children is noticing how each child's developmental themes repeat themselves. Once you understand, for example, *why* a six-year-old loves riddles, you'll also understand why a game of peekaboo isn't interesting anymore. Such insight allows you to go beyond such common and meaningless explanations as "She's outgrown it" or "He's only going through a stage." (Unless I specifically state otherwise, all references to boys apply equally to girls, and vice versa.)

Throughout the text I have scattered case histories and guidelines. Almost all the case histories tell the story of an individual child. For a few I've taken the literary license of combining the experiences of several children into a single case.

More important than the content of this book is its spirit. The topics I have included are by no means comprehensive. Just as a good cookbook may inspire amateur chefs to try new ways of approaching common foods, I hope this book encourages adults to look at children from a new perspective and to try some of these techniques in novel ways.

I also hope parents use this book as an excuse for making mistakes and for allowing their children to make mistakes. Without such mistakes there is little learning. Too many parents are convinced that if they do something wrong, they will somehow warp their children's personalities and undermine their competence. If research on the ability of children to cope with very stressful situations has shown us anything, it is that they are more emotionally resilient than we ever imagined. They are also more forgiving. Children do not shatter like spun glass. They bounce.

No book can teach you how to avoid making mistakes in raising children. My hope is that this book will give you additional insight and skills to help you cope with some of the most common and frustrating challenges you face as a parent. You won't stop arguments, but you will argue more effectively and about different things. Your child won't quit testing your limits, but you will understand those tests and be better skilled at responding to them.

Raising children is not a competitive sport. A certain amount of competition is inevitable, for we all feel a touch of pride when our child learns to walk a few weeks earlier than her cousin did or masters the intricacies of fractions ahead of most of her classmates. While pride in the accomplishments is justified, competition on such matters between parents or children is unfair to both parties—especially to the children.

Invariably when I speak to groups of parents, someone asks me whether the trouble he or she is having toilet training a child is a sign that something is wrong. It almost never is. What concerns me, however, is the competitive approach parents take to this and to other developmental landmarks. They are carrying around a mythical standard by which they measure their children's competence.

I usually begin my response to that question by asking for a show of hands of those parents in the audience who have not been successfully toilet trained. (I live in fear that someday someone will raise his or her hand.)

I vividly recall how one woman, who spent her professional life as a trial attorney, described in great detail how she was losing a prolonged toilet training battle with her two-and-a-half-year-old daughter. The woman was feeling understandably frustrated. Much of that frustration, however, came from her focusing only on the act of toilet training, not on the other ways in which her daughter was developing and, not coincidentally, showing that development through her temporary refusal to follow her mother's instruction in this matter.

In addition to feeling upset over the toilet training, for which the girl was apparently not yet ready, the mother could have felt justifiably pleased by how well her child was learning about the uses of power. Despite her small size and limited resources, she had found an extremely effective way of driving home a powerful point about her desire for independence. I kept thinking how the girl, if she kept it up, might turn into an attorney just like her mom.

My point is that rather than get into a panic, try to relax about the situation and gain some perspective. That perspective comes by your understanding what children are saying both through their words and through their actions. It comes by your expecting and accepting your feelings of frustration and anger as much as you do your feelings of pride and excitement. It also comes by your not expecting yourself to be perfect or even close to perfect.

Being a parent is such serious business that we dare not take it too seriously. Children are inherently funny. So are parents. We all are at our funniest when we are desperately struggling to appear to be in control of a new situation. (It took a few episodes for me to learn that a particular cry from our infant son was an announcement of impending bladder activity rather than a complaint about a wet diaper. I hesitate to recall how many times I unwrapped him, only to have him immediately wet my clothing instead of his own.)

A few weeks ago I watched my brother-in-law, who is a registered nurse, and his wife try to change the diaper on their one-day-old son. He's their first child. It took the two of them several minutes to accomplish the task. They discussed strategies, rehearsed techniques in midair a few times, argued over the relative merits of covering and uncovering the child between diapers, and then finally went about this very dramatic and prolonged diaper change. I'm convinced that after two weeks either one of them could change their son's diaper while half asleep, alone, in the dark, and with one hand tied behind his or her back. They have gained a perspective on diaper changing and, more to the point, their new roles as parents.

Childhood is an adventure both for children and for their parents. There should be freedom to explore and joy in discovery. The important discoveries for both parents and children seldom come at the points where the path is smooth and straight. It is the curves in that path to adventure that make the trip interesting and worthwhile. We should welcome them.

CHAPTER 1

The Myth
of the Perfect Parent

GOOD PARENTS make lots of mistakes. So do good children. Yet for at least four generations we've been told precisely the opposite. The result has been a great deal of anger and frustration for both parents and children.

Raising a child is probably the most daunting task a person can undertake. The problems, both real and imagined, actual and potential, are by their very nature overwhelming.

The joy, on the other hand, can be indescribable. One of the main things that interfere with our joy is the belief that if we try hard enough, read the right books, follow the right advice, and buy the right things, we could be perfect parents. If we are good enough as parents, our children will be perfect, too.

There is a certain appealing logic to that belief. It's deceptively straightforward and uncomplicated. It imposes a structure on what often appears to be a chaotic situation. Armed with all this information, we try to do the things that will give our children the best lives possible. If reading by age six is good, then reading by age four must be better. If having a computer at home can help a high school student, it will also be a real advantage to a second grader. If we treat our children with the right amount of love, they will never reject us.

But when parents try these things, they often find the four-year-old still can't read, the second grader pays little attention to the computer, and the thirteen-year-old finds them painfully embarrassing to be with.

Unfortunately, what comes from trying to live out this philosophy is not perfect children but worried parents. We feel as if we have failed. What are we doing wrong? How do we sort through the well-intended but often conflicting advice we get from neighbors, friends, and relatives? How can we strengthen our relationships with our children? How come other parents don't seem to have these problems with their children?

Much of the time parents aren't doing anything wrong, and in fact, the other parents who we assume are handling things so well are having exactly the same difficulties. The problem lies in failing to understand what's happening as our children grow. The parents' expectations of themselves and of their children are out of alignment with their children's development.

One of the greatest sources of frustration for parents is the myth that other parents are naturally "good with children," that they have innate knowledge and skills that allow them to deal with their children in an intuitively brilliant manner. It makes us question our competence at times when we really need re-assurance and support. The source of this myth for at least the past few generations can be traced to the distorted ways in which families and relationships have been portrayed in the mass media. These distortions have played a large role in molding our expectations for ourselves, our relationships, and our children.

Novels, magazines, radio, television, and films permitted us, when we were children, to learn about family life and relation-ships by reading about, listening to, and watching a wide variety of fictitious families. Romance novels and magazines showed us the passion, power, and glamour of untainted love. Popular children's books, be they about the Hardy Boys or Nancy Drew, often showed us talented, problem-free children who were con-sistently supported by their families and who regularly showed themselves smarter than adults. Radio programs and motion pictures often showed the same pleasant distortions.

For the current generation of parents, the most persistent bearer of this false message has been television. Images of perfect parents pervaded the programs that today's parents watched as they grew up in the 1950's and 1960's. Early television was populated by implausible families that reflected some writers' beliefs about what America either was or would like to be. Fathers knew best. Mothers were housewives obsessed with milk and cookies. The master bedrooms contained twin beds separated by a respectable distance. Sex, politics, death, money, illness, stress, drugs—the very issues that punctuated the lives of real families then and still do today—all were conspicuously absent.

While the teenagers in film families of the fifties were shown as rebels without a cause, the children of television families are better described as rebels without a clue. These TV children were blissfully naive. Their problems were portrayed as cute rather than painful. They threw no tantrums. They were not exposed to drugs. They never questioned their sexual identities. Their parents could help them out of any difficulty by saying the right words—words those parents seemed to know instinctively.

There is an insidious quality to this portrayal of family life. As children we envied the members of these fictitious families. We were unsophisticated enough to believe such perfect families could exist. Not only that, but they probably lived just down the block. Our own families, with illnesses and deaths and concerns over money, were obviously the unusual ones. Our parents, who lost their tempers, drank too much, or were even divorced, must be far outside the norm.

But television's love affair with the perfect parent did not end in the 1960's. The plots of family programs now involve more realistic issues. Parents are sometimes divorced. Children are members of stepfamilies. Adolescents, and occasionally even their parents, are sexually active. Both mothers and fathers hold jobs. Children make decisions about drugs. But still, the parents appear to have ingenious solutions to every problem the children suffer.

While television of the 1950's, at least in retrospect, appears heavy-handed and even laughable in the way it presented messages about being a parent, more recent programs may be conveying those very same unrealistic messages with more sophisticated packaging. *The Cosby Show,* the most popular and one of the best situation comedies of the 1980's and 1990's, presents an image of the family that is at least as unattainable to the typical viewer as the blissful harmony of *Father Knows Best* was in the 1950's.

Both parents on *The Cosby Show* have advanced academic degrees and work as professionals. The mother is an attorney; the father is an obstetrician. All the children are attractive and precocious. They live in what is obviously an expensive house in a friendly and safe, racially integrated neighborhood. Everyone gets along with all the relatives and has lots of time to spend with the children. There are never any serious financial problems. Nobody loses control of his or her emotions. No one ever has to use the bathroom. The house apparently cleans itself and does its own shopping.

Although the social setting has changed, the presentation of both parents as being able to solve their children's problems instinctively and on the first try has remained. These television parents are perfect. They are powerful, brilliant, rich, loving, and all-knowing. Their children are apparently above average on every measurable dimension. Unlike the larger-than-life protagonists of ancient Greek drama, these parents have no fatal flaws.

I grew up in a family that looked and felt very different from the "perfect" families I saw on television and read about in books. I was adopted as a newborn infant by a couple in their forties. My father, a widower whose first wife had committed suicide, was a politically conservative entrepreneur and a small-time landlord. My mother, a divorcée whose first husband had painted backdrops for burlesque houses, was a former union organizer with strong socialist beliefs. Political discussions were as much a part of dinner as dessert.

Although both my parents were warm and loving, not all my relatives shared those traits. My paternal grandmother's first words upon seeing me when I arrived home from the hospital nursery were "He's too puny. Send him back!" That set the tone for our later relationship.

My father became ill when I was five and died when I was eight. My mother and I moved in with other relatives, a mismatch that led to years of bickering and an eventual separation of the two groups. Life at home contained financial troubles, jealousy, sickness, and depression as well as love, excitement, passion, and pride. As I look back on it, it was much more stressful and infinitely more interesting than growing up on *Leave It to Beaver* or *Ozzie and Harriet*.

It was obvious to me, even as a child, that the television family members were actors reading scripted lines that they had rehearsed. But to this day I still find myself using such television programs as a small part of my frame of reference for how I should behave as an adult and what I can give to and expect from children. The television families of our childhood showed us people who could do it all and do it perfectly at a time when we believed such things were possible. The television families of our adulthood reinforce that belief in the perfect parent.

And so as adults we feel guilty and frustrated and inadequate when we cannot measure up to this standard. We do not know that simple phrase that will instantly comfort a crying pre-schooler or help a teenager make an important step toward independence. But it is the standard that is false. The illusion of television is so powerful that we forget, at some level, that the children's responses are determined by the writers and that the real arguments occur off camera. The illusion of books is so strong that we forget that the stories are crafted for us as readers and not lived by the protagonists. We willingly suspend our belief and occasionally forget that it's all been make-believe.

Nowhere is the belief in perfect parenthood more strongly, if unconsciously, stated than in the words used to describe the families of divorce. We say that the marriage has failed. It is as if the relationship were a matter of quantum mechanics. It exists in one state or another: Success or failure, perfect or irredeemable, with no possibilities in between. What are children to think about themselves as the products of such failures? How are parents to succeed at being a father or mother if they have "failed" at being a husband or wife?

Divorced parents decide on the custody of their children and on parental visitation. Yet "custody" is a word most often associated with prisons, and "visitation" usually involves paying respects to the dead. These are strange words to describe what should be a lifelong sharing relationship between parent and child. They reflect our ambivalence toward this unattainable goal of perfect parenthood.

The Reality of the Imperfect Family

Picture the typical American family for a second. The odds are your image is wrong.

One of every four children in the United States lives with only one parent—a significant increase from 1960, when it was one in ten. The numbers are even larger among minorities. Approximately 53 percent of black children live with only one parent, as do 30 percent of Hispanic children.

Approximately 60 percent of today's children will spend some time in a one-parent household before they leave home. For two out of three of those children, they will live with one parent following their parents' divorce or separation.

One in six children under eighteen lives in a stepfamily. By the year 2000, according to government estimates, that figure will rise to one in four.

The "nontraditional" family is rapidly becoming more common than the two-parent family we all imagine to be typical. Even among those families in which the children live with both their biological parents, the dad-at-the-office-and-mom-at-home image has been largely supplanted by families in which both parents hold down jobs. Child care outside the home for infants and toddlers is not a matter of choice for many families; it is an economic necessity.

All this means that many of the pressures you face as a parent are different from the pressures your parents faced. The family environment in which your children are growing up is different from that in which you grew up. The decisions our parents made and the strategies they used were developed in a different context from what we face today, even if the "content" of the problem is the same. It is a mistake to think that our own experience as children and adolescents will give us all we need to help our own children. The rules of the game have changed.

One of the most critical elements of being a successful, if imperfect, parent is developing effective ways to communicate with and listen to our children. Although there are guidelines, there are no simple formulas for successful parent-child communication. The magic words that television parents utter work only because the children's responses are already in the script. Doing the things our own parents did is no guarantee of success. Rather than blindly repeat (or reject) our parents' behaviors and take (or ignore) our neighbors' advice, we must see how well the things they did fit with the environment in which our children grow up today.

Developing Your Own Philosophy of Child Rearing

None of this is simple. Parents receive a great deal of wanted and unwanted advice from relatives, friends, and neighbors. While some of the specifics, such as activities that will keep a toddler occupied or techniques for encouraging a child to do homework, can be very helpful, your fundamental approach to child rearing is something you must develop by yourself. What values do you wish to instill in your children? How will you handle discipline, rewards, and punishments? What do you consider private information that you will keep from your children? How will the roles of mother and father be different? If you're a single parent, what extra responsibilities will you assume?

That personal philosophy of child rearing is the compass that will guide you through the confusing and often conflicting information you will hear and read from child development professionals, well-meaning relatives, and other parents. It is a philosophy that should be and will be constantly reassessed and frequently changed, if only slightly, as you come to know more about yourself and your children. It is a philosophy that will allow you, in times of crisis, to step back and say to yourself, "Wait a minute—does this make sense?" and to act accordingly.

Developing such a personal philosophy sounds more daunting than it actually is. Dr. Benjamin Spock's famous comment at the beginning of *Baby and Child Care,* "Trust yourself. You know more than you think you do," is still very sage advice. It's far too easy to become so overwhelmed by the details of child development and so overawed by alleged experts that you lose sight of the fun.

Go ahead, make some mistakes. Revel in them. They're perfectly normal. I've noticed that when parents attend parent education classes or seminars, one of the most important insights they often come away with is that other parents have made the same mistakes and have the same difficulties that they have. What usually starts off as one parent's hesitantly admitting her or his frustration with a problem often turns into a competition over which parent in the room has the most frustrating child. The haze of tension that blanketed the room begins to lift. Soon a parent describes something good a child has done. The other parents join in with their stories. It is a ritual that bonds them as a group and allows them to cast off their feelings of isolation.

Such workshops are often wonderful catalysts for encouraging parents to question their own and their partners' assumptions about child rearing. Many spouses have different parenting styles. The mother may be very open and expressive; the father may be more stoic and emotionally constrained. Each may be making false assumptions about what the other is feeling. There is nothing inherently wrong with having a different approach to child rearing from your spouse's, as long as you're comfortable with the differences and can agree on ways to handle conflicts. Too many parents try to hide evidence of conflicts from their children. Aside from being a hopeless endeavor, since children are extremely tuned in to their parents' stress levels, having all your battles behind closed doors deprives your children of the opportunity to learn ways of handling frustration and conflict.

You should, of course, expect your children to be acutely aware of your differences and to try to play each of you off against the other. If Mom says that bedtime is 9:00 P.M., Dad may say that it's 9:30 P.M. A child who can convince his father to buy him a toy boat but not a toy airplane and convince his mother to buy the airplane but not the boat will often end up with both toys. Such ploys are both very common and undeniably irritating.

Rather than simply get mad at your children for doing such things (it is, after all, a highly adaptive skill) or rather than give in to their manipulations, congratulate them on their skill at family politics, defer your decision, and take the time to discuss with your spouse whether you should regroup and form a more united front. This is, admittedly, much easier to propose on paper than it is to do in the heat of the moment. Even so, looking for the adaptive qualities of such frustrating behaviors can make it easier to cope with them.

When forming your personal philosophy of child rearing, remember to take the time to celebrate. Although most parents marvel at their baby's first words and first steps, there is as much magic in a preschooler's first joke or a teenager's increased use of the telephone. The word and the step are celebrated as rites of passage to full status as a human being. But parents who are not aware of the significance of the more subtle signs of development miss out on the joy of celebrating these steps toward adulthood.

In some ways, being a parent is like being an anthropologist who is studying a primitive and isolated tribe by living with them. Children operate within a different culture from that of adults. A four-year-old with an imaginary friend is considered cute; an adult with an imaginary friend may find himself being questioned by a local psychiatrist. The courtship rituals of teenagers cruising through shopping malls rival the colorful mating displays of puffed-out pigeons strutting before one another in the local park. To understand the beauty of child development, we must shed some of our socialization as adults and learn how to communicate with children on their own terms, just as an anthropologist must learn how to communicate with that primitive tribe.

Discovering ways to communicate effectively with children requires that parents understand the cultural and developmental differences not only between adults and children but also between children of different ages. For example, a toddler who sees a playmate who has fallen down and is crying will sometimes react to that situation by kicking or punching the injured child. Children this age have few ways in which they can express the tension they feel. Hitting the crying playmate is often not an expression of anger or malevolence toward the injured child; it is simply one of the few ways the toddler can express the upwelling of strong emotions he or she is feeling. It is, in effect, a demonstration of the child's developing sense of empathy, for a younger child would not have felt the frustration that came from identifying with the injured playmate.

Even after they become more skilled in verbal communication, children are much more concrete in their use of language than adults are. Idiomatic expressions, such as "I'm sorry, but I lost my head," can be confusing or even frightening to a preschooler. A five-year-old niece of mine recently asked me what the focusing knob on the slide projector did. I told her it made the pictures on the screen sharper and asked her if she wanted to try turning it. She said that she was scared to turn the knob because she might cut herself on the sharp pictures. It was a mistake that her younger brother would not make because he does not understand the word "sharp." It was a mistake older children or adults would not make because they understand the figurative meaning of the word.

What Happened to the Good Old Days?

Why all this emphasis on understanding child development? After all, children have been growing up without all this psychology stuff for thousands of years. Why don't we return to the simplicity and old-fashioned values of the past?

There are even more myths and misunderstandings in this area than in the image of the typical family. Despite the romantic appeal of growing up in a quaint revolutionary era town like Williamsburg or whitewashing fences and rafting down the Mississippi like Tom Sawyer and Huck Finn, the realities of an old-fashioned childhood are about as attractive to a child as old-fashioned health care would be to someone with acute appendicitis.

Such myths color our perceptions of what is "right" and "natural" in the lives of children. We assume, often subconsciously, that the concept of childhood that was accepted when we grew up and that we take for granted has been around for a long time. We also tend to view childhood stress as a relatively recent phenomenon. Understanding the history of childhood, especially over the past few hundred years, gives us a new and very useful perspective that helps us develop our own philosophies of child rearing.

Let's step back for a moment and look at the fundamental assumptions we make when we use the word "child." The concept of childhood that we all take for granted is actually relatively new. Although infancy has always been seen as separate from adulthood, that bridging period we now call childhood was not as clear. Many of the modern symbols of childhood were absent until about two hundred years ago.

In Western and many other civilizations, children didn't wear clothing that was different from that of adults until the early nineteenth century. Compulsory schooling was unknown, as was the distinction between juvenile and adult crime. The thought of a child who did not work was as strange an idea as retirement.

In the United States the abstract notion of child welfare did not become a topic of popular discussion until the social reform movements of the late nineteenth century. Even so, the perception of children as a protected class came as a bit of an afterthought. The same people who founded the American Society for the Prevention of Cruelty to Animals also founded the New York Society for the Prevention of Cruelty to Children. The children's organization, however, was incorporated nine years after the ASPCA opened in 1866.

Theories of child development and guidelines for parents are not cast in stone. They are constantly changing and adapting to new information and new pressures. There is no "right" way, just as there are no magic incantations that will always painlessly resolve a child's problems.

Inevitably parents will disagree on what's right for their children. Such disputes should be embraced rather than avoided, for they can lead to a better look at the context in which their children are growing. Such statements as "When I was a kid, we always did it this way!" can be seen as the often weak arguments that they are.

And so we, like every other generation of adults, must go about the task of reinventing parenting in ways that reflect the environments in which our own families are developing. To create a philosophy of child rearing, we must understand the objectives and limitations of our roles as parents. To do that, we must understand the changing and fundamental goals of the child.

CHAPTER 2

Windows into a Child's Mind

THERE IS an orderly structure to child development. But it is not like the structure of a skyscraper with each floor built solidly upon the one below it. The growing child is more like a symphony. Each aspect of the child's emerging personality takes the lead in its turn, sometimes alone, sometimes in concert with others. The melodic themes of childhood modify and repeat themselves within this structure, gaining complexity and elegance as the child grows older.

As with music, a quiet, slow period of development can communicate as much as a loud, fast one. The tempestuous interactions of different behaviors can, with practice, often be reduced to easily recognized and simple themes.

There are certain fundamental goals or tasks of childhood that drive many of these behaviors. Foremost among these goals is growth, not only physical but emotional, intellectual, and social growth as well. Nutrition will, within reason, take care of the physical growth. Emotional, intellectual, and social developments are more challenging because their patterns within children are, as far as we know, uniquely human.

By the time we reach adulthood we take for granted some of the most complex and difficult information a child struggles to understand. Individual identity is a good example. Not only must infants learn to recognize their parents, but they must arrive at the realization that they are separate individuals from their parents—a concept that often puzzles developmental psychology students. Once children understand that they are individuals, they begin to learn that they are also part of a group, such as a family or a school class or a play group. They must also realize that they are the same as the other members of those groups in some ways but not in others. With this come the development of empathy and a tolerance of differences.

The yardsticks by which we measure these and other aspects of a child's growth are often complex and obscure. Formal intelligence tests and observation by trained psychologists or physicians can help determine the areas in which a child's development is on track. For most parents, such tests are not necessary. Children will constantly tell us where they are developmentally if we learn to look for the proper information.

Knowing what to look for and how to interpret a child's behavior is almost always very reassuring to parents. Although parents realize that children are different from one another in their abilities, many parents underestimate how broad a range of behaviors is considered "normal." Much of the variation between children, such as when a child learns to sit up, reaches puberty, or goes out on a first date, is really of little consequence. It is much more important that a child learn to read, to cite one example, than whether that skill at reading comes when the child is four, five, six, or even seven years old. The fact that a child passes through a developmental milestone is almost always much more significant than the age at which he or she passes through it.

That variation in each child's development and skills is part of the beauty of childhood. Biographies of famous men and women are replete with tales of children who did not learn at the same pace or behave the same way as their peers. Charles Darwin was reportedly a terrible student. Eleanor Roosevelt was painfully shy and withdrawn as a child. When Winston Churchill was a boy, he was described as disobedient, intellectually dull, and an uncoordinated weakling. Thomas Edison was constantly getting into trouble as a child and was removed from school by his parents after only a few months. Yet it was their very deviance from the norm in other areas that eventually made these renowned people interesting and successful.

Parents who assume that a child who speaks or walks or reads earlier in life than another is somehow "better" than the other child are missing this key idea and, more to the point, are probably worrying themselves needlessly. Research by Dr. Anne C. Petersen at Pennsylvania State University has shown that adolescent boys who reach puberty later than their peers have lower self-concepts than their classmates when they enter high school, but higher self-concepts than those same classmates by the time they are graduated. The apparent problem quickly turns into an advantage.

Look for Stages, Not Ages

Books on child development almost always include a chart of some sort outlining the normal milestones of child development. Parents can look up the ages of their children and see what they should be able to do. A nine-month-old, according to the typical chart, will show a fear of strangers and can hold her own bottle. Such charts often include a note explaining that parents should expect and accept as normal a certain amount of variation in the ages at which children can perform the tasks described. The fact that the information is in a chart and that it involves numbers, however, works against that warning, for we expect charts and graphs to be inherently more precise than words alone. Taking such charts too literally is as much of a mistake as ignoring them.

Holding a bottle and becoming fearful around new people are behaviors that do not magically develop on the first day of the ninth month of life. (In fact, there's evidence from several studies that the fear of strangers that parents were told to expect from their nine-month-olds does not appear at all in a significant number of infants.) If these developmental markers show up a month early or a month late (as the child gets older, that latitude should increase to up to a year or more early or a year or more late), it's usually no big deal. The patterns of development are much more important than the precise timing.

This is not to say that such charts or guidelines are useless. Quite the contrary, they help orient us to the patterns of child development and warn us of possible problems. If, for example, an infant cannot hold a bottle by the time he's a year old (i.e., well past the average age at which most children do this), you probably should see a pediatrician about the problem. If a child still can't read by the end of second grade, you should insist on his undergoing some testing for learning disabilities and getting special help for him before the problem becomes more difficult to solve.

The developmental patterns presented in typical charts of physical development can also be seen throughout the universe of children's behaviors. The stages of physical development are fairly clear-cut and readily observed. Newborn infants will show what appear to be random but symmetrical movements of their arms and legs. During their next stage of development, which usually occurs somewhere around six months of age, they will begin to reach for specific objects with their arms. A few months after that they will have enough control of their hands to use them as pincers for picking up small objects. Somewhere around one year of age most children can reach for small blocks or rattles, pick them up, and, if they're in the mood, give them to you if you hold your hand out.

Language shows similar discrete, if fuzzy-edged, stages of development. Within three months or so, most infants will progress from only crying to a form of cooing or making certain simple vowel sounds. The ability to form consonants, especially the sound *mmm*, comes a few months after that. (Children who say "mama" before they say "dada" may be telling us more about their neurological development and coordination than about their preference for a parent.) After a few more months they usually respond to their name and certain frequently heard key words such as "NO!"

Somewhere around one year of age the child will start using words, especially nouns. After another year or so the child will know a couple of hundred words and will be able to tell you the names of some objects in picture books—a very important step since a picture of a dog or a chair is very different from a real dog or chair. By the time children are ready for preschool they know about a thousand words and will soon begin saying complex sentences such as "You can watch me draw a picture."

Similar stages may be seen in psychological development. Issues such as fears change in a generally predictable pattern as the child gets older. Infants often dislike loud noises, being poorly supported while they're held, and being uncovered. Within about nine months to a year they may become anxious when their mothers or other caretakers leave them alone and when they see strangers. By the time they're toddlers their fears focus on things they can see and hear, such as dogs or thunder. Preschoolers have more sophisticated fears that reflect their growing understanding of their own bodies and of abstractions. They insist that cuts and bruises be covered by a bandage and, if one of their parents is around, kissed "to make it better." They worry about ghosts or being kidnapped by pirates or other bad men. These are fears of abstractions since unlike the dog or the thunder that frightened them earlier, pirates and ghosts don't have to be seen or heard to be frightening. Such abstract fears often continue until adolescence, when they are replaced by fears that reflect their self-concepts. Teenagers worry about failure and embarrassment—concepts that would have made little sense to them a decade earlier.

Telling a preschooler that she shouldn't be afraid of ghosts or a teenager that he shouldn't be concerned with what other people think is fruitless. Such statements deny their developmental accomplishments. Being afraid of ghosts when you're four years old is, in many ways, something to be proud of. It is a demonstration of the child's developing intellectual capabilities. Similarly, being acutely aware of social awkwardness at age thirteen reflects the child's growing skills at empathy.

The most commonly described developmental markers, such as when a child first sits up, says a complete sentence, or goes out on a first date, reflect only a tiny fraction of the important physical and social changes children are constantly undergoing. Although we attach importance to such developmental milestones, we largely do so because they are easy to observe. Looking for some of the more subtle changes can, quite frankly, be a lot more fun. Unfortunately, children don't come to breakfast in the morning and say things like "Hey, Mom and Dad. I now understand the concept that objects can be classified in more than one way." Such realizations, which as adults we take for granted, are equally important to a child's development.

Yet children do tell us when they reach these less obvious milestones. The ways in which they give us that information, however, are often cryptic and require that we shed some of our adult assumptions if we are to decipher them.

Looking for and interpreting these clues are among the greatest joys of parenthood. The stories children tell, the things they fear, the games they play—all provide a window through which we can glimpse their developing minds. To dismiss their behavior as simply childish is to do it a great disservice. Being scared of strangers at twelve months of age or acting defiantly at age two are not simply benign stages through which a child passes on the way to becoming an adult. They are as much a sign of normal development as is toilet training or learning the alphabet. Often, subtle behaviors actually give us more insight into a child's growth than the obvious milestones, like learning to walk or saying a first word.

Humor as a Clue to Development

The things that children find funny tell us a great deal about their level of development and what is on their minds. There is a connection between the two-year-old who bursts into a fit of giggles upon hearing the nonsense phrase "bottle, battle, bittle" and the young adolescent who laughs at the bawdiness of an off-color joke.

The specific things children laugh at tell us which developmental tasks they are struggling with. That is a pattern that runs throughout childhood. It explains why three-year-olds, who are often still mastering toilet training, are enthralled by "bathroom" humor while seven-year-olds, who no longer consider toilet training an issue, think such jokes are just stupid.

Laughing and smiling are among the most human of behaviors. A twelve-hour-old infant will shape his mouth into what looks like a smile at the smell of a banana or other sweet food. Our nervous systems appear to be wired to make us smile. No learning or imitation is needed. True laughter, which is more complex, does not appear until a few months later.

Children learn some very complex things during their first dozen months, starting with the realization that they are separate individuals from their parents. Soon they begin to understand that objects and people exist, even when they are out of sight. This is a very profound realization. When Mom leaves the room, she is doing something else and will eventually return. A toy that is placed behind a cardboard barrier can be obtained if you reach around or over the barrier. By reaching for that toy, the child shows that he understands the concept that people and things have a physical existence even when they are not seen. (The first time I tried this test on my six-month-old son he tried to eat the cardboard barrier!)

Few things elicit as much laughter from a one-year-old child as a game of peekaboo. Yet a six-month-old will barely respond to the game, and a six-year-old will find it boring. Laughing at peekaboo is a marker for a certain level of intellectual development. The intensity of the one-year-old's laughter tells you that he or she "gets it": That's my mother behind those hands! It is a realization that would have eluded the child only a few weeks or months earlier.

The game of peekaboo still works if done in silence. Watching the mother's face disappear behind her hands excites the child, who knows that the mother is back there and predicts that she will reappear. It is a tense situation. When the mother's face comes back into view, the child is relieved and laughs with excitement. What was scary is now fun, for the child can predict the future. If the mother keeps her face hidden for too long, however, the child's tension will turn to fear, and the child will cry.

Once children understand a concept, they take great joy in playing with it. Two-year-olds who are beginning to master the intricacies of language will giggle uncontrollably when they hear a combination of words and nonsense syllables. They understand that the nonsense syllables are different from the words. The sounds are out of place. They are funny.

Other things that are out of place will get the same laughter from two-year-olds, for they are learning that there is an order to the world. Placing a sock on a foot is not funny. Placing it on an ear is hysterical to two-year-olds because they realize that it does not belong there. They share their mastery of that knowledge through laughter.

Children at that age may also tell you for the first time that they are being silly. Unlike the younger child playing peekaboo, the two-year-old with the sock has controlled the stimulus for laughter. The child has made a joke.

A six-year-old child no longer finds peekaboo and socks hanging from ears as funny as they once were. The challenge and the tension of those tasks have been replaced by a newfound appreciation of logic and abstractions. The riddles and jokes of a six-year-old often contain ludicrous juxtapositions, plays on words, or logical flaws. "Why did the elephant paint her toenails red?" "So she could hide in the strawberry patch." "What did the baby ghost say to the bully ghost?" "Leave me alone or I'll tell my mummy!" "What's the best month for a parade?" "March." They are simple versions of the humor we enjoy as adults.

The content of these jokes reflects the six-year-old child's struggles with the intricacies of logical thought and growing facility with language. The elephant that thinks she will blend into a strawberry patch by taking on one superficial aspect of it does not understand something that the child now understands. It is a funny image to six-year-olds because they can imagine and identify with the elephant that is trying in vain to hide. The small child knows more than the big elephant. With that knowledge comes power that can be flaunted.

The ghost and parade jokes make use of the child's increasingly sophisticated skills with language. "Mummy" sounds like "mommy," but it is not a random association. The baby ghost is calling upon a larger and stronger being for protection, just as the child would. The child has used wordplay to conquer something frightening (a mummy) and transform it into something protective (a mommy). Similarly, the parade joke allows the child to display mastery of the idea that one word can have several meanings. That is a very difficult concept, one that younger children cannot fathom.

The innocent tone of children's jokes changes before they leave elementary school. For reasons psychologists do not fully understand, by the fourth or fifth grade boys laugh at different things from those that girls do. By the time boys are ten years old, they are telling jokes that are very physically violent and very sexual. Girls at that age like humor that is less physically but more verbally aggressive, perhaps because they have, on average, better verbal skills than boys. They tease each other about boyfriends and act like caricatures of the vamps they see on television soap operas. The jokes help define membership in a particular social group. Those who get the joke belong to the group; the others are outsiders.

Despite the apparent differences, both boys and girls are using humor to accomplish the same goals. To young adolescents, humor is an indirect way of coming to terms with the issues of greatest concern to them, such as their sexuality. An eleven-year-old boy who laughs at a joke about prostitution or abortion is not necessarily making a judgment about either issue. They are far too emotionally stressful for him to deal with directly. Instead, he uses the joke as an opportunity to determine cultural norms and acceptable behavior. It offers him a chance to try out a position and, if necessary, retreat from it quickly.

Parents as Detectives and Diplomats

Communicating effectively with a child often requires that a parent combine the deductive skills of Sherlock Holmes with the boundless tact and patience of an ambassador. Throughout the remainder of this book I will try to give you some tools and fresh perspectives that I hope will help you become a more effective parent. Two of the benefits of this increased knowledge should be more fun and fewer worries.

I can guarantee you, however, that things will not go easily. Children have an innate ability to bring out all sorts of extreme emotions from their parents, including incredible amounts of frustration. Actually this shouldn't be surprising. Your children have studied you more intently than anyone else has. They know exactly how to push the buttons that trigger your emotions. The child who did not know how to get his or her parents' goat would be a disappointment, as would the child who did not know how to extract a needed hug.

The first few times a child screams at you, "I don't want you.

I want Daddy [or "I want Mommy"]!" can cut you to the quick and bring about all forms of self-doubt. It's still a bit mysterious why a twelve-year-old one day will curl up affectionately next to you on the couch and the next day will be unwilling to speak to you through the closed door of her room. A fourteen-year-old may appear bored and uninterested when you talk about sex, even though he is listening intently. Knowing that such behaviors—and many others that bother parents—are usually normal, not a reflection of your parenting skills, can help you weather the storms.

Being aware of what is normal will also help you spot things that are abnormal more quickly and act on them more effectively. A five-year-old's fear of attending a grandparent's funeral may reflect some basic misunderstandings about death. An eight-year-old may not be willing to tell you about his fear of a bully at school and, in fact, may vehemently deny the problem. A teenager who does very well in school but is always dissatisfied with her work may have a serious and growing problem with perfectionism.

The topics in this book are by no means exhaustive. Children are forever composing new variations on the themes of childhood. With a bit of work, however, you'll begin to recognize many of the melodies within your own children.

Remember, don't expect perfection, relish your mistakes as well as your discoveries, and have fun. After all, you'd want your children to do the same.

CHAPTER 3

Transitions

YOUR FIVE-YEAR-OLD girl cries as you wave good-bye to her on the first day of kindergarten. Your nine-year-old son is troubled enough by nightmares that he is developing insomnia. You receive a confusing phone call from your eight-year-old at sleep-away camp asking if the family dog is still alive. Your four-year-old daughter insists on taking her own pillow with her when she sleeps over at her grandparents'. Your toddler suddenly starts demanding more attention while you're packing the boxes for your move to a different house.

Although the situations and the children's behaviors are different, a common and extremely important thread connects them all. In each case, the child is having difficulty with a transition.

Transitions are among the toughest challenges for both children and their parents. It does not matter if the transitions are apparently good, such as being promoted from kindergarten to first grade, or apparently bad, such as being cut from a school sports team. Transitions of all sorts are, by definition, stressful. It is this layer of stress that makes interpreting the behaviors of and communicating with those children during times of transition so important and, all too often, so difficult.

The ways in which children approach the dramatic and even routine transitions in their lives, and their early success at handling change, can have a large effect on their attitudes and perhaps even their accomplishments as adults. This shouldn't be very surprising. After all, one of the ways we judge other adults, such as co-workers and government officials, is by the speed and ease with which they adapt to new and challenging situations. We often use the same basic approach to judging children as well, describing those children who go off to kindergarten without crying, for example, as "more mature" than those who shed tears. This may not be the case, however.

Some transitions, such as going to sleep or meeting new people, seem routine and are often ignored. Others, like going to day care or summer camp or moving into a new neighborhood, are more likely to be noticed. Several of these transitions are predictably difficult. Many preschool children feel safer entering the world of sleep if their bedrooms have night-lights. Coping with nursery school may be less stressful if a child takes with her something that reminds her of home—what psychologists call a transitional object.

Understanding the stress and challenge of transitions can be one of the most powerful tools available to parents. When a child is upset or otherwise having problems, it's often useful to analyze the situation by looking for the stressful transitions in that child's life rather than to focus on the end points. A sleep problem is frequently better seen as a going-to-sleep problem or a waking-up problem. Academic difficulties at the beginning of junior high school sometimes signal an adapting-to-different-teachers problem.

Yet seldom will children express their problems in such terms. Their words and behaviors are often symbolic rather than direct, for children often do not have the words to tell you or even themselves what they are feeling. Noticing the nature of the transitions your children are facing will often give you insight into the solution to their problems or, often more important, let you know when they're nothing to worry about. The power of this approach can be clearly seen by looking at a transition that, at first blush, appears to offer little in the way of communication between parent and child. Through careful observation, however, the language of sleep, especially the transition to sleep and to wakefulness, even among infants and toddlers, becomes clear.

The Art of Going to Sleep

Although it appears so deceptively simple that we take it for granted, learning to go to sleep is often as much of a challenge to children as learning to walk. Bedtime is a cue for frustration for many parents and children. Babies cry when they wake up in the middle of the night. Toddlers refuse to leave their families' evening activities to go to sleep. Preschoolers ask their parents for yet another story or drink of water or trip to the bathroom. Older children become frightened of ghosts or monsters that climb into their rooms when the sun goes down.

Sleep problems are among the most common difficulties of childhood. They affect about one in four children, according to Dr. Richard Ferber, director of the Center for Pediatric Sleep Disorders at Children's Hospital in Boston. These problems may be as benign as a brief bout of insomnia or as dramatic as repeated sleepwalking or night terrors. A child's difficulty sleeping is, in a sense, contagious. Because few parents can sleep well when their child is up during the night, sleep problems are a common reason parents seek help from pediatricians and psychologists.

For some children, the problems start soon after they are born. During their first eight weeks many infants fall asleep while they are nursing or bottle feeding. Usually their parents carefully put them to bed without awakening them. In some cases such apparent kindness may be doing the children a disservice, for those babies learn to associate the presence of a parent with the act of falling asleep.

When they wake up in the middle of the night and there's no adult around, they become frustrated. They're unsure how to make the transition to sleep by themselves, so they cry until someone comes. The parent picks the child up and, by doing so, inadvertently perpetuates the problem. The child falls asleep in the parent's arms but is still unable to fall asleep alone.

The key issue here is not sleep, although that is how parents will usually refer to it when describing the problem. The baby is sleeping just fine. The problem lies in mastering that transition from the waking state to the sleeping state. Once parents realize that, possible solutions to the problem become more apparent.

One deceptively simple approach, recommended by Dr. Edward R. Christophersen, the director of the behavioral pediatrics section of Children's Mercy Hospital in Kansas City, is to look for times during the day when the child is awake but drowsy. Put the child to bed, quietly leave the room, and let her fall asleep by herself. This doesn't mean that you should never let your child fall asleep while nursing or being held. What you want to do is help the child learn to fall asleep in a variety of situations so that she does not feel she needs someone else to be present. If she's mastered that skill, waking up alone in the middle of the night is less of a cause for concern for her. She's felt drowsy and alone during the daytime. She knows what to do. She falls back asleep without crying—at least most of the time.

Sleep problems may occur in children during times of stress. Infants sometimes develop problems sleeping when they have colds. Stuffy noses may make them uncomfortable at night, causing them to wake up crying a few hours after midnight. Parents, who are acutely aware that their children are suffering, go to their rooms to comfort them.

This sleep problem may persist, however, for a few weeks after the cold is over because the parents keep going into the child's room at 1:00 A.M. when they hear a noise. It's an understandable reaction on the part of both the parent and the child. The parent is being protective; the child is getting extra attention. Often the extra attention, which was appropriate while the child was sick, has made the child dependent on the presence of a parent in order to fall asleep.

One approach to this problem, recommended by Dr. O. J. Sahler, a behavioral pediatrician at the University of Rochester, is quick and effective, although initially bothersome to most parents. If you're 100 percent sure there's nothing wrong with the infant, simply don't respond to his late-night cries. That's a very painful decision to make, for it is both physically and emotionally difficult to tune out your baby's cries. Recognize, however, that the infant simply has to relearn how to make that transition from wakefulness to sleep by himself. This usually takes three or four nights at most. If the problem isn't solved within that time period, see a pediatrician.

Toddlers often need help shifting gears from the animated activities of the day to the more passive pursuits of bedtime. Parents frequently assume that children can mentally prepare themselves for bed as quickly as adults do. They need a cool-down period. If Daddy's just played horsey with them, it's too abrupt a transition to go to bed.

Rituals form an important part of this cool-down period for toddlers and preschoolers. Quiet activities, such as being read a story or listening to soothing music, can help the child learn to fall asleep without problems. Television, however, is not good for this since it is filled with rapid-fire images that are too stimulating. The bedtime story or glass of milk becomes the child's transitional object for entering sleep. That's one of the reasons why preschoolers will often ask to have the same story read to them for weeks or months at a time. It provides reassurance that all is well and that they will be safe when their parents leave them alone for the night.

Preschoolers will often test the limits of their bedtime by stretching those rituals with requests for additional stories or drinks. The bedroom becomes a battleground in the fight for attention and control. Clear-cut but realistic rules for bedtime are especially important. Remember that one of the things preschoolers are looking for when they test these limits is whether they can predict their own safety. Rules provide them with a sense of order and predictability that can be very reassuring.

Requests for "just one more thing" can also simply be demands for extra attention. Bedtime, of course, is not a good time for this extra attention, which is better given during the day, when both of you are in better physical and emotional shape. Remember that arguing with the child over these issues at bedtime may be counterproductive since the argument provides the child with at least as much attention as the extra glass of water. It is better, in the long run, to have clear rules for bedtime that can be discussed only during the day.

Preschoolers and even school-age children sometimes become fearful at bedtime. Those fears reflect the growing sophistication of their intellects. For the first time their minds are developed enough to handle abstractions. They can imagine what it would be like to be kidnapped by pirates or attacked by monsters, yet they are not sophisticated enough to put those fears in perspective. Simply telling a child that such fears are silly is of little help. They are scared of losing the protection their parents offer them and of entering the unknown darkness of sleep.

Even though children will eventually rid themselves of these unrealistic fears, they can be very stressful for both parents and children when they occur. Night-lights can help, as can leaving a flashlight by the child's bed for her to use if she becomes frightened. The object, of course, is to empower the child by giving her the ability to handle these fears without relying on the presence of her parents.

Rituals can also be very useful in helping children who are scared of the dark. One successful approach taken by some parents is to buy an empty colored spray bottle from a local pharmacy or department store, and to label it ghost spray or monster spray. You can either leave it empty so that all it sprays is air, or you can put some water in it. Children lightly spray their bedroom windows and perhaps under the bed before going to sleep to keep evil creatures away. Since you're only using air or water, it's perfectly safe and won't do any damage if the child accidentally sprays himself.

Another helpful ritual is a poem, song, or story the child can say to herself. Many children find comfort from even the simplest incantation, such as "Jane is a brave girl. Ghosts and monsters are scared of her. They stay away from her bedroom. Everything is fine." The advantage of such a chant, of course, is that it's eminently portable, works equally well at any time of night, and, unlike spray bottles filled with water, won't run out when it's needed the most.

Quick Tips for Sleep Problems

There are several general guidelines for parents in helping children overcome their sleep problems.

- Remember that you can't control your children's sleep. You can control only their bedtime. If a child says he can't sleep, tell him that he has to be in bed. He can read. He can listen to music quietly. Usually the child will doze off in a short time.
- Not all children require the same amount of sleep at a particular age. While some children are groggy if they don't get as much as nine hours of sleep per night, others are happy with as little as six hours. Often toddlers who have trouble sleeping through the night can change that habit by taking fewer and shorter naps during the day.
- Pay attention to when your child falls asleep. If a child goes to bed at 7:00 P.M. but always falls asleep at 8:30, you might be better off putting him to bed at 8:30. There will be less of a struggle at bedtime, and the child will get the same amount of sleep.
- One of the most common reasons toddlers have difficulty sleeping through the night is that they nap too much during the day. If that's the problem, substitute some quiet play or listening to music or a story for some of the nap time. This is, of course, more easily said than done if your toddler is attending a day care program since nap time is often one of the few breaks a child care provider gets during the day.
- If you want to teach your toddler or preschooler new skills having to do with falling asleep, such as learning to go to sleep in a strange bed, introduce those skills during daytime naps rather than at night. Young children perceive more dramatic differences between night and day than do adults. Daytime is much less mysterious and frightening than nighttime for these children and is therefore a less stressful time to try new things.

• Encourage calming rituals around bedtime. Remember that children often need at least ten minutes to calm down from the excitement of the day. A warm bath or a cup of hot chocolate is often effective.

Clues from the Unquiet Night

Another difficulty faced by many young children is understanding the transition between the reality of wakefulness and the fantasy of dreams. Toddlers and preschoolers live in a magical world populated by omnipotent and omniscient parents and mysterious happenings. To a young child, there is no reason to assume that the dragons and witches of fairy tales don't live down the block. If cartoon characters can fly when they're on television programs, real people should be able to do the same. The problem with this poor ability to distinguish between reality and fantasy occurs when children have disturbing dreams. Unlike adults, who can usually brush off their frightening emotions by assuring themselves that what they felt and saw were only nightmares, children have trouble making that transition back to reality. Yet it is that very difference in the way they react to dreams that makes looking at childhood sleep so interesting.

Children can tell us a great deal about their development even when they are asleep. In fact, wishing that someone sleep like a baby may be more of a curse than a benediction. The brain of a sleeping child works differently from the brain of a sleeping adult. There is a link between the three-year-old who sleeps so soundly that he does not wake up when you carry him from the car to the house and when you get him undressed for bed and the toddler who frightens the whole family with his screams of terror a few hours after he goes to sleep.

The patterns of childhood sleep and dreams offer insight into how children learn to control their bodies. Two of the strongest clues lie not in sweet dreams but in nightmares and night terrors—incidents that sometimes distress parents more than they bother the children who have them. By understanding the difference between those sleep problems, you can often help your children control their nightmares and separate fantasy from reality.

A child's brain appears to be wired for dreaming even before birth. Several sleep researchers have recorded the patterns of brain waves we associate with dreaming in a child's very first nap after birth. The content and structure of those early dreams—if, indeed, they are dreams—are unknown. The infant obviously does not have the language to tell us what he imagines while he sleeps. Yet even at an early age we can see these two types of sleep disturbances in almost all children.

A nightmare is simply a dream gone bad. It has a plot with a twist that is frightening. Most children's nightmares occur early in the morning. The child will wake up scared and upset. If he can talk, he will tell you what frightened him in the dream. He will cling to you for comfort and respond to your reassurances.

Night terrors are quite different. Although almost all children will have at least one mild night terror, patterns of severe or repeated night terrors appear to run in families. They usually occur within a few hours of falling asleep. A four-year-old having a night terror may sit bolt upright in his bed with his eyes wide open and scream. He may call out for his parents, yet he doesn't recognize them when they come into his room. When they try to hold him and comfort him, he pushes them away as if escaping from a trap. The fighting and screaming may last as long as half an hour. If his parents ask him later what frightened him, he cannot tell them. In fact, he may not even remember being scared.

Night terrors are not dreams. The screaming child with the open eyes and swinging arms is still asleep. In fact, he is in the deepest state of sleep, a condition parents usually notice only when their toddler or preschooler falls so soundly asleep that he does not wake up as they prepare him for bed.

This very deep sleep is a sign of how well developed the child's nervous system is. As the child matures, he loses the ability to sleep through anything. It appears to have another important role in a child's development, for it is during this deepest stage of sleep that the child's body produces much of the hormone that controls his growth.

Night terrors may be seen in children as young as six months. Most parents pay little attention. At that age children simply appear to be sleeping restlessly and may thrash about in their cribs. Night terrors are most commonly seen in preschoolers. Almost all children outgrow them by the time they are six or seven years old.

Quick Tips for Night Terrors and Nightmares

Young children are more likely to have night terrors when they are very tired. Despite how frightening they may appear to the parent and how terrified the child appears to be at the time, night terrors are usually nothing to worry about, unless the child flails about so much that he may hurt himself.

Among older children, night terrors are often triggered by medical problems, such as pain caused by an ear infection. If a school-age child has a night terror for the first time, the child should be seen by a pediatrician. Similarly, if a child who had night terrors as a preschooler experiences several terrors within a few weeks as an older child, the child should be brought in for an evaluation.

There is a paradox in helping a child who has had a night terror. Since the child is asleep throughout the episode, trying to reassure him at the time is fruitless. All that parents can do is gently restrain the child, if possible, so that he cannot accidentally injure himself. Once the child is awake, he won't remember what scared him, so he doesn't need your help. In fact, questioning him the next morning about what happened may only make him anxious.

Nightmares, on the other hand, are more likely to be triggered by emotional distress than a physical problem. Again, they are usually of little concern unless they always have the same theme or occur more than about once a week.

One way to help a child who has had a nightmare is to ask the child to draw a picture of what frightened him. (Do this the morning after the nightmare since at the time it occurs, neither of you is functioning at your best.) Without trying to analyze what it means—an effort that is probably beyond your child's understanding anyway—you can ask him how he could defeat the monster the next time or whom he would like to take along for help if he had the dream again. By drawing and talking about what scared him, the child learns that he can master his fears. Some children even learn to confront the monsters that chase them in their nightmares and to ask them what they want.

One other successful approach is to tell young children who are bothered by nightmares that dreaming is like watching television inside your head. Most of the programs playing are lots of fun. But if you're scared by what you see, you can always change the channel. A surprising number of children can teach themselves to do exactly that.

Transitional Objects

Part of the fascination of childhood is the way in which children are able to communicate their feelings and needs without words. Their behavior constitutes a language rich in texture and subtle in meaning. Although many of their acts are direct, such as grabbing cookies when they're hungry, some of their most profound statements are symbolic. The preschooler who starts wetting the bed again soon after his baby sister is born, for example, is expressing clearly and dramatically how much he wants his rightful share of the family's attention.

Transitional objects are among the most powerful symbols in children's lives. By observing how their children use them and, equally important, when and how they abandon them, parents can gain a great deal of insight into the developmental challenges those children are facing. Transitional objects, represented by the ever-present security blanket carried by Linus in the *Peanuts* comic strip, are important tools for most children and often a cause for concern by parents.

To an adult, the object clutched in the child's tiny hands may look like only a grubby blanket or a tattered doll. Or it may simply be the child's own thumb wedged securely between her teeth. To the child who is relishing its comforts, however, it is much more. Just as the presence or touch of a parent may help an infant go to sleep by easing that transition from wakefulness, so may people or articles aid children in facing other threatening or challenging situations.

The ways in which children use these transitional objects tell us a great deal about their development. In most cases using transitional objects is normal not only for young children but for adults as well. After all, we each have a favorite shirt or other article of clothing that feels especially good because of the memories or associations it holds. Many adults go through a particular ritual before going to sleep, such as plumping the pillow, reading a book, or curling up into a particular position. These are our transitional objects, the cues that help us control how we feel. We never really give up transitional objects. We simply become more sophisticated in using them.

The doll or swatch of cloth an infant or toddler holds so close is perhaps the child's first crude attempt at symbolism. She has learned that a parent can be comforting during times of stress and now, as she faces the world more independently, must learn to comfort herself. The transitional object, which is often something that was present when the child was being cared for or fed by her parents, acts as a stand-in for those parents when they are out of sight.

Almost all children use transitional objects of some sort, especially during times of stress and before the age of five. With some it is obvious, such as the two-year-old child who drags a stuffed animal she brought from home along the floor of her new day care center. With others it's more subtle—a favorite pillowcase that eases the child into sleep. In fact, the inability of a young child to use an object for self-comforting may be a sign of problems that require professional help. Instead of clinging to a blanket when facing a stressful situation, such as time spent away from their parents, these children scream, withdraw, or otherwise fall apart emotionally.

Obvious transitional objects, such as blankets and dolls, are most common among children below the age of three. Almost all children start using more sophisticated ways of coping with stress by the time they enter the first grade. One reason for this change is peer pressure. A preschooler sees other children in her class who are handling things without their teddy bears.

She wants to be like them and, therefore, takes the risk of leaving her bear at home or in a corner of the room.

Children should not be expected to give up their transitional objects all at once. Although parents expect children to regress a bit in their behavior when they are faced with significant changes, such as a new sibling, a move, or a change of schools, the stress that causes a preschool or early school-age child to reach once again for a transitional object need not be as obvious. Children may need a transitional object at night for a few years after giving it up during the day. It is easier for children to cope with stress at times other than bedtime. It's also easier for them to cope when there are other people around than when they are alone.

Many parents are confused and sometimes embarrassed by their child's constant embrace of a doll or blanket that, to put it mildly, could use a thorough washing. Yet the child resists having it taken away and, if it is washed or replaced, immediately gets the new object dirty again. Realize that it's the smell, the texture, the very dirt of it that comforts the child. That's why substituting a brand-new version of the same thing doesn't work.

Using and Giving Up a Security Blanket

Learning to use transitional objects can be a very important step for a child along the path toward independence. If two- and three-year-old children have difficulty separating from their parents, it's often useful for those parents to provide their children with objects that they can take with them to their baby-sitters or day care centers.

One item that works particularly well is a small clip-on teddy bear. (Any similarly soft and small item will do.) The parent (in this case, let's assume it's the mother) should wear it for a few hours and show the child that she is doing so. If the mother usually wears a particular perfume or cologne, it sometimes helps to spray a very small amount of that fragrance on the bear. (Fathers can do the same thing with their aftershaves or other scents, if they use them.)

When the mother separates from the child, she can give him the bear and tell the child that when he misses her, he can hold it and stroke it. When they get back together at the end of the day, the child can give it back to his mother to wear for a while so that the bear gets "recharged."

Weaning an older child away from a cherished blanket or doll requires that parents acknowledge the symbolic importance of the transitional object. Simply taking the object away will seldom work. Instead, try offering the child new and more satisfying things. This may take a few tries until you find the right combination. For example, you may be able to help a child go to sleep in a new house by telling him a story or by teaching him to tell himself a story.

If the transitional object is a blanket, it's often useful to cut off a small square of that blanket and give that to the child for comfort. Usually the size of the object is of much less concern to the child than its texture and smell. This process can be repeated over a few weeks until the child no longer needs the small piece of cloth.

Parents will sometimes be concerned if a two-year-old becomes very attached to a doll that has lost its head or is accidentally deformed or mutilated in some other way. Usually you should not read too much into the relationship. Remember the child's focus on smell and texture rather than sight. Don't assume that a headless doll carries the same symbolic meaning to a two-and-a-half-year-old that it does to an adult. Take your cue from the child as to whether it's disturbing. If your child isn't anxious about the change, you probably shouldn't be.

Braving the Outside World

Transitional objects are not the only symbols through which children convey their willingness and ability to separate from their parents. The behaviors as well as the words of children as they imagine or test themselves in new environments tell us how ready they are and what types of support they need to make these challenging transitions to maturity and independence.

The self-reliance and self-confidence children develop during their early years can have benefits that last well into adulthood. Going away to college, moving away from home, and starting a first job can be emotionally similar to the experiences of young children facing the challenges of kindergarten or sleep-away camp. They can be viewed as opportunities for success, chances to fail, or measures of the person's worth. They can be exhilarating or terrifying. Understanding the ways in which children of different ages show their concerns can help parents provide the specific support and guidance that these children need, which may last them a lifetime.

The steps children take toward feeling comfortable away from their parents are usually small, starting with a few hours in a day care center or a day spent with grandparents or other relatives. Especially stressful for many children, however, are their first experiences away from home for an extended period. Often these take place during a week or even up to two months spent at a summer camp.

Although the examples I give in this chapter focus on summer camp, the children's emotions and the recommendations for parents could just as easily apply to other new situations for children. Summer camp offers children a chance to test their independence and their ability to cope with a new environment. Those are the same basic tests children face when they move into new neighborhoods or enter new schools. The skills they learn in handling one will help them handle the others.

Within a few weeks of the beginning of summer, thousands of parents receive tear-stained letters or telephone calls from small, choked-up voices saying something like "I'm miserable. Everyone at camp hates me. I wanna go home!" Yet not all children become homesick the first time they're away from their families for more than a few days. The way a child is prepared for a first summer at camp may be more important than the child's personality or even age in determining whether he'll be homesick. In many cases a child's homesickness may be prevented or, at the very least, reduced if parents take a few simple steps in the weeks before camp starts.

The more a child knows about a camp before he goes, the

more likely he'll adjust well. Find out the daily schedule from the camp director, and go over it with the child. Knowing a few details of what to expect every day, such as what time mail from home is delivered and that milk and cookies are served every afternoon at three-thirty gives the child a sense of control during his first few days at camp. This sense of control lowers the likelihood of homesickness.

Seeing some familiar faces on the first day away from home may ease the transition. Ask the camp director to have your child's counselor write him a letter and include a picture a week or two before the season begins. Arrange for get-togethers with nearby families whose children go to that camp.

A new camper who has never spent time in the country can have some very frightening fantasies about the hidden dangers of summer camp. To an eight-year-old, the woods of New Hampshire may be filled with lions and tigers. The small lake in the Poconos may harbor a distant relative of Jaws disguised as a three-inch sunfish with very sharp teeth. Scary campfire stories the child may have heard from older children who've come back from camp or scouting trips don't help the situation. Ask the child about the animals and people he pictures living in the woods and in the lake. By gently correcting his unrealistic images, you can reassure him without belittling his fears.

Although you should talk to the child about what homesickness might feel like, be sure to explain that it goes away after a day or two. In some ways, simply talking about homesickness and putting it in perspective appear to inoculate a child psychologically against becoming homesick. The feelings of longing are much less disturbing if the child knows that they're normal and that they don't mean there's something wrong with him.

Examine your own feelings about your child's leaving for the summer. Homesickness is often as much the parents' problem as it is a child's problem. Parents who are concerned or upset about their child's going away send subtle and often confusing messages to him. The child, of course, wants to accommodate his parents' wishes and may therefore think that he'll be a disappointment if he does not become severely homesick. Let your child know that even though you'll miss him, you expect him to have a good time.

Talk to your child about the successes he will have at camp, but be careful not to put pressure on him to perform to a certain standard. It's often better to say, "Won't it be great when you can show us all around and introduce us to the people you've met?" than "You'll be able to show us how you've learned to swim and to ride a horse." If the child is nervous about meeting your expectations, he'll have much more trouble adjusting to camp.

As the departure day approaches, some children start saying they don't want to go to camp after all. Often a child's nervousness about leaving home may mask a larger concern that he is embarrassed or afraid to discuss unless a parent brings up the topic. One of the big issues for children is a fear that they will be humiliated or put down by people they don't know. Talk to the child about the successes he has had in other new situations, such as going to a new school or joining the Boy Scouts. Other, less rational beliefs, especially among very young children going to camp, are that family members or pets will die while they are gone or that parents will abandon them. If your child still appears uncomfortable for no apparent reason about going to camp, it's sometimes useful to ask directly about these issues and to offer reassurance about them.

Two final techniques can help lower the likelihood or the severity of homesickness. Have a letter from you waiting for your child when he arrives at camp. In it, encourage him to try new things and remind him how often you'll write. Also, don't buy an all-new wardrobe for your child. Remember the power of familiar clothes as transitional objects. The memories stored in an old pair of jeans or a T-shirt with a grape juice stain from a family picnic can help a child face and overcome his fears.

When Homesickness Is a Sign of Something Serious

Most cases of homesickness start as soon as the child leaves for camp. It usually disappears within a few days. The plaintive cries of "Come pick me up now!" are best met by telling your child that you know he's upset and reassuring him that things will soon get better. If the teary letters and phone calls last more than ten days, it may be a sign that something more serious is going on or that the child is not ready for the stresses of sleep-away camp.

Call the camp director and the counselor and ask what's going on. Does your child have friends? Is he included in groups? Some children think their parents will be disappointed if they're not homesick, so the stories they tell don't reflect what's really happening. Reassure the child that it's OK to be independent and to have a good time without Mom and Dad.

If a child develops homesickness halfway through the session rather than at the beginning, that's a red flag that something isn't right. This timing often indicates that the child is feeling overwhelmed, very upset, or threatened. Occasionally these midseason cries for help are a sign of emotional or physical abuse. Reassure your child that you won't be upset with him for telling you what's scaring him.

The most common reason for picking up a child early from camp is that the child is emotionally too young for the experience. Remember that children can feel very humiliated by this and take an inordinate amount of responsibility for failure. Reassure your child that maybe next year he'll be ready.

Moving

Moving to a new house may be very traumatic for children. Unlike most other transitions in a child's life, moving is an act that involves the entire family. Parents, who often feel appropriately overwhelmed themselves with the moving preparations and the prospect of numerous changes in their jobs and lives, may miss or misinterpret some of the signs of children's distress. The potential for problems related to the move is increased when the move is due to another change in the structure or status of the family, such as a death, divorce, remarriage, or significant change in finances.

One family I spoke with described their children's responses like this: Weeks before his family even started packing, the five-year-old boy began running aimlessly around the house.

When he was with adults, he would try to capture all their attention. His twelve-year-old sister, however, showed no obvious anxiety and even told her parents that she looked forward to the move from Oklahoma to Illinois because it was "a neat thing to do." She acted as if she had everything under control. But as the moving day approached, she became more obstinate when her parents or teachers asked her to do something. She began overreacting to ordinary events. A sad song on the radio or a curt word from her parents triggered her tears.

After the move, and despite his parents' patient and repeated explanations that the family now lived in this new place, the boy spent several months telling them that he wanted to go home, meaning back to Oklahoma. The girl's school grades dropped during the next semester, as did her self-esteem. Within four months, however, all those problems cleared up, and the family was back to normal.

The stress of moving to a new home, whether it is down the block or across the country, is felt most acutely by those who did not make the decision to move. Generally, the family members who have the least control over where they live, and are therefore most likely to react poorly to a move, are the children. Many parents worry either too much or too little about the effects of a move on children. Studies have shown that a certain amount of emotional turmoil or depression is normal and may even be beneficial.

The increased activity that the young boy showed before the move may have been triggered as much by biology as by psychology. Studies of preschoolers done by Dr. Tiffany Field, a psychologist with the department of pediatrics at the University of Miami Medical School, have found that those children who were about to move or change schools typically went through a period of agitation and then depression. They had a more difficult time falling asleep, woke up more during the night, showed changes in their blood chemistries, and were more likely to get upper respiratory infections. That pattern is very telling, for it is similar to the responses of monkeys that are separated from their mothers. Dr. Field and other researchers think that the depression that usually follows the period of agitation among both highly stressed monkeys and children may be adaptive since it prevents them from becoming exhausted and, in the case of the children, allows them to cope with the stress of the move.

For older children, the key issues appear to be how well and how quickly they adjust to their new schools. Studies such as those by Dr. Thomas J. Berndt, a developmental psychologist at Purdue University, show that most children have relatively few problems making this transition. Those who have the most difficulty are usually children who also had trouble at their old school. In general, it appears that boys have more trouble adjusting to a move than girls. Junior high school students have more difficulty than any other age-group. Children who move from small elementary schools to large junior high schools appear particularly vulnerable to problems.

Usually a few weeks or even a few months of lowered grades or complaints about not fitting in after a move are nothing to worry about. If a child is still having difficulty adjusting to a new school after six months, that's probably a sign of a more serious problem that requires professional help.

Helping a Child Adjust to a Move

The moving van is the harbinger of summer. Nearly one in five families living in the United States moves, during a given year, with more than 40 percent of those moves taking place between June and September. Here are some ways to help children adjust to their new homes and schools:

• As moving day approaches, reassure toddlers and even preschoolers that they will be coming along with their parents on the move. A surprising number of young children see their family's possessions being boxed, sold, or thrown out and wonder whether they will suffer the same fate.

• Put off redecorating your children's new rooms for a few months unless they ask you to. Having the old furniture arrangement is like taking a security blanket. It eases the transition to the many other new things they are facing.

• Pay attention to the ways the design of your new home influences how you spend time with your children. The increased privacy of a larger house can sometimes make it harder for children to adjust. The new home may not have the same type of central family gathering place, such as a combination kitchen and dining area, as the old one. You may not realize you're not spending as much time together as a family as you used to.

This problem may be compounded if family members have different schedules from those they had before, so that it's more difficult to eat dinner together. For the first few months after a move it's often useful to schedule family meetings or other all-family events as a way of maintaining lines of communication.

• Ask the school to arrange for a "buddy" in the same grade who can show each of your children around the school for the first week or so. This gives your children a kind of temporary membership in a social group and alleviates a lot of stress while they try to figure out where they fit in.

• If it's at all possible for one of the parents to delay returning to work for a few weeks, do so. Knowing that Mom or Dad will be at home if she or he is needed may make some of the changes your children face appear less threatening.

• Following a divorce or the death of a spouse some parents move for emotional rather than financial reasons. In those situations, if you can at all keep from moving, don't move. It's often too much for the children to cope with. The children may need to keep some of the memories you're trying to leave behind.

CHAPTER 4

Self-concept

In a public service announcement on national television a teary-eyed girl flinches as she hears her parents call her stupid and clumsy. A few seconds later a young boy smiles proudly as his parents tell him what a good job he's done. The message is clear. Children learn who they are by how we label them. Your child's self-image—her mental photograph of herself—is a reflection of what you say to her. One child is doomed from the start; the other will grow up to be a winner.

If only it were that simple. A parent's influence on a child's self-image is more likely to be subtle and unconscious than the name-calling shown in the television spot. A child's self-image is more like a scrapbook than a single snapshot. As the child matures, the number and variety of images in that scrapbook may be far more important than any individual picture pasted inside it.

Children constantly send out messages asking how they are regarded by others. Most of those messages are symbolic or oblique. "If I do something that I know is dangerous, will I be protected?" "If I cry, will I be comforted?" Many mothers have watched their toddlers or preschoolers fall down and scrape their knees without uttering a whimper. Yet as soon as those children see their mothers, the crying starts. Clearly such crying is more a test of the mothers—and indirectly a test of the children's worth—than it is a direct result of the pain from the fall.

Developing a favorable and resilient self-concept is one of the major tasks of childhood. Much of the role parents play in this process is deceptively subtle and a far cry from the image portrayed in the public service announcement. The ways in which parents communicate with their children, as well as the content of those countless messages, are perhaps the major force in shaping children's self-concepts. Those words and actions have a powerful effect that reaches well beyond childhood. The self-images developed during childhood form the core of the images and beliefs we have about ourselves as adults. Only by understanding this complex and convoluted process, and the important role parent-child communication plays within it, can parents best help their children to mature as self-reliant and confident adults.

The Path to Self-esteem

Infants and toddlers are lucky they don't judge themselves by the standards of adults. Would adults keep trying to learn a new language if, after months of work, they couldn't say a single word? How many of us would simply smile and pick ourselves up after waddling headfirst into the leg of a chair?

A child's first three years are laced with more failure than he would emotionally tolerate by the time he is five. That change is marked by the child's development of a self-concept—labels and feelings that quickly become as much a part of the child's identity as his name. It is an image of himself or herself that the child will carry into adulthood.

One of the first tasks in forming that self-concept is differentiating between doing something badly and being someone bad. It is a learned skill that is hindered or helped by how parents talk to their children. Some studies indicate that it is more difficult for young girls to make this distinction than young boys. This sex difference appears to continue into adulthood. Interviewed about their activities and emotions, women report feeling more shame (a judgment of themselves) and men report feeling more guilt (a judgment of their behavior) when describing things they've done wrong.

There's some evidence that part of that difference between the sexes may be traced back to the way their parents talked to them before they were three years old. Developmental psychologists at the Robert Wood Johnson Medical School in New Jersey have noted that parents who are helping their toddlers use different words when talking to boys from those they use with girls. The comments to their sons were mostly about the task—statements like "good job" or "I like the way you put that piece in the puzzle." Daughters, however, were more often told things like "You're such a good girl!"—evaluations of them as people rather than comments on what they did. Other studies have shown that teachers often unconsciously fall into the same pattern.

The problem, as far as self-esteem is concerned, is the usefulness of the information. If you tell me (a child) that I have done something well or poorly, I can use that information to adjust my behavior to improve. I can also use that information to reach the conclusion that I should feel proud of what I've done. The next time I do that task, whether it is stacking blocks, reading aloud, or washing my hands before eating dinner, I can evaluate my own performance and, this time without relying on your judgment, feel good about what I've done. If I show up next week for a meal and have dirt on my hands, not only do I know that that's not acceptable behavior, but I also know how to correct the situation and I'm confident that I can correct it.

On the other hand, if all you tell me is that I'm a good boy or a bad boy, I don't know what to repeat or what to change. I am dependent upon you for evaluations of my work. It's much more difficult for me to reward myself for a job well done. I must look to outsiders for their opinions to know how I am doing. I may know that having dirty hands at the dinner table is wrong, but I don't have the information to know what's right or whether I can make it right.

This is not to say that parents should not tell their children that they are good boys or good girls. Quite the contrary. Every child needs to hear those sweet words. However, it helps to mix such praise with specific comments about the things children are doing well, so that they can practice the more sophisticated task of judging themselves. Keep in mind that it's almost always more useful for children to hear what they're doing right than what they're doing wrong.

Another difficulty faced by some children has less to do with the specific labels they apply to themselves than to the number of those labels. An active preschooler who is repeatedly told he's a troublemaker may get caught in the cycle of making trouble for the teacher to get the attention he needs. It is the only approach he knows will work. His self-image becomes crystallized around this one aspect of his behavior.

Studies of children this age conducted at Yale University show that those who have too limited a range of beliefs about themselves do not adapt well to elementary school and other new situations. They have significantly more difficulty learning to read and write than their classmates.

Children who have more multifaceted self-images, which may include believing that they are artistic, inquisitive, funny, and thoughtful as well as troublemakers, are much more adaptive to change. If something they try doesn't work in the new situation, they have other approaches they feel comfortable using.

Although a four-year-old who keeps telling you that he's a bad boy is sending clear signals about trouble with his self-concept, many children give off much more subtle messages. Sometimes the children who are no problem to their parents should be looked at more closely. This is especially true if those children are extremely obedient and have few friends their own age. A good self-concept allows children to explore the world, risk engaging in conflict and failing. Children who play it safe by never disobeying or risking conflict may be telling you that they feel unqualified to face the world head-on.

A Matter of Semantics

As children become more fluent in their speech, we often assume that they know far more about the words they use than they really do. By looking closely at the ways preschoolers and toddlers speak to us, we can learn where they are in figuring out how the world works.

For young children, using language is a constant experiment. If you say something and you get what you want, you'll say the same thing the next time you want it. A four-year-old who learns that when she says, "May I please have some ice cream," she is more likely to get it than when she simply says, "I want some ice cream," is learning little or nothing about politeness, no matter what her parents think. The concepts of politeness and protocol are beyond her intellectual abilities. To a child that age, the word "please" is little more than a magic charm that increases the efficacy of her self-centered requests. That's why young children will whine and repeat the word "please" and adults and older children, who understand the idea of politeness, do not. The young child who wants the ice cream is parroting the word because she associates it with both the situation and the outcome she desires.

Parents should be careful when they assume their children are using words in the same way as adults when those children are referring to their self-concepts. Dr. Jerome L. Singer, a professor of psychology at Yale University, illustrates this point by telling the story of a four-year-old girl who started dragging her feet toward the end of an afternoon walk with her father. Finally the girl stopped, looked up at him, and said, "Carry me, Daddy. I'm spoiled!"

Reshaping a Poor Self-concept

One of the first signs that children are having difficulty with their self-concepts is a concern over some physical attribute. Almost all children, at some point, say they don't like something about the way they look. "My nose is too big!" "I wish my ears didn't stick out!" "I'm too fat!" Why does the same nose that a parent finds cute loom so large in a teenager's mirror? Why do children choose a particular time to say something about them is wrong and should be fixed?

There are times when children's statements that they are fat or ugly are obvious cries for reassurance that they are worthy of love and that their roles in the family are safe. But often there is a hidden message. Rejecting their physical appearance may be a safe way for children to explain to themselves larger problems in their lives.

One of the most common triggers for self-deprecating comments is the divorce of the child's parents. A young child is likely to assume that if his parents split up, it must be because there's something wrong with him. While some children will talk in terms of "never being a bad boy again," for others the thought that they might have been able to prevent the breakups is too threatening. They are caught in a double bind. Since the divorce, they believe, is their fault, they have failed. If they could have done something to stop it yet did not, they have failed even more miserably. They therefore decide that although they were responsible for their parents' divorces, it was for reasons they could not control. They were too short or too ugly or had red hair. Parents who readily dismiss such apparently outlandish claims by their children are often accidentally reinforcing the very thing the children fear most: that they are both culpable and powerless.

Such self-deprecating statements may also reflect the way children interpret how their parents view themselves. Pediatricians and psychiatrists regularly report seeing children who are not obese but who believe they are too fat. Often these children come from families in which one or both parents are concerned about their own weight. The children have simply internalized the parents' concern as a normal state of affairs and have accepted it as what they should be feeling. "Adults say they want to lose weight. If I say that I want to lose weight, then people will view me as more of an adult."

Parents' offhand comments like "I can't do anything with my hair!," "I can't go out without my makeup on!," or "You have to be tough to survive in this world" may have the same effect, especially since children often interpret such comments literally and without the cultural assumptions adults bring to understanding them. (Financial writer Andrew Tobias recounts how he earnestly told a preschooler, "It's a dog-eat-dog world out there," only to have the child beam with delight as he repeated the words he thought he heard: "It's a doggy-dog world! It's a doggy-dog world!")

Among older children and teenagers, self-deprecating comments may be a sign that they are uncomfortable with something they're feeling that's completely unrelated and that they don't know how to handle these strong and often conflicting emotions. Rather than express their discomfort or confusion directly, they turn it inward. Their frightening feelings become transposed onto their faces or bodies. It is easier for a teenager to say and, more important, to believe that his nose is ugly than to admit the "ugly" feelings of anger he has toward someone else.

When a Child Says, "I'm Ugly!"

Here are some guidelines to use in helping children who complain that they are unattractive:

• Recognize that many children won't tell their parents when they feel ugly or inept out of fear that their parents will support those conclusions. When children do make self-disparaging statements to their parents, it usually means that they're ready to talk about other things that are bothering them.

• Begin by accepting your child's feelings rather than refuting them. If you say, "That's ridiculous! You're beautiful!" the child will probably stop talking and shut you out of his or her emotions. Although the aim of such comments is to make the child feel better, by unintentionally belittling the child's emotions, parents may give a message that the child interprets as meaning that even her most heartfelt and painful emotions are not recognized by her parents.

• On the other hand, don't agree with the child too

quickly. If a boy complains that his nose is too large, replying that he can have it fixed when he gets a bit older will simply reinforce his belief that there's something fundamentally wrong with him. Instead of making the child feel better, it makes him feel terrible. Think of it this way: If a child said he thought he wasn't lovable, what parent would respond by saying, "Let's wait a few years and then see if we can do something to make you more lovable"?

• Ask the child why his or her ears or nose or weight is a problem. Did someone say so? Has the child just been rejected for something else? Is the child anxious about a coming event like a school dance? Often simply allowing children to express their feelings—without your trying to fix the problem—is enough to make the concern go away.

• There are some adolescents who have valid concerns about their looks and for whom cosmetic surgery can make a significant difference in the way they perceive themselves. The problem is determining ahead of time which children will benefit. One clue appears to be how realistic the child is about the short-term physical and social changes expected from an operation. A child who believes that a reshaped nose alone will bring new popularity may develop more serious self-image problems if this unrealistic goal is not instantly achieved.

Self-concept and Sexuality

Many parents feel uncomfortable discussing sex with their young children. Yet sexuality is an intimate part of a child's self-concept from a very early age and a large part of the communications between parents and children. Much of what children learn about their own sexuality and the sexuality of others comes from the ways their parents behave, not from what their parents say. The sexual values and beliefs that express themselves forcefully in adolescence and adulthood are rooted, in part, in children's early concepts of themselves.

Teaching children about sexuality and sexual responsibility may and does start at a very young age. The methods parents use may, at first glance, appear to have little to do with the topic. The subject may be introduced well before a child can understand sexual reproduction. In fact, the mechanics of sex are probably the least important aspects of sexuality that children learn. None of the bad outcomes of sexual activity that we fear as parents, such as rape, child abuse, other forms of exploitation, unwanted pregnancy, or sexually transmitted disease, comes about solely because of the mechanics of sex. They all involve issues related to how people feel about and treat others and how they handle issues of responsibility. Far more critical to children than learning the details of intercourse at a young age is understanding that they should think of others as independent and worthwhile human beings. It is especially important that they learn to think of themselves as worthy of the respect of others and capable of making their own decisions, for that self-concept will inoculate them against many forms of sexual exploitation when they become older.

Children as young as two years old can be told and shown why parents take care of babies. It is an introduction to how adults feel responsibility for other people. Grade school children need to learn about respecting other people's values when they are different from their own. Should you force another child to do something simply because it's what you want to do? Again, the content doesn't have to be sexual for the child to learn the lesson.

The plots of television programs older and more sophisticated children watch and the lyrics of the songs they listen to can be springboards for conversations that are directly related to sexuality. What might happen if those two characters wound up in bed? What does she find attractive in that man? What do those lyrics mean to you? Does that make sense? How would you feel in that situation? Would it make a difference if you were the woman or the man?

Sometimes it's useful to talk with more than one child in your family at once. Eight-year-olds will often ask the questions that teenagers are afraid to ask, since teenagers will try to appear more sophisticated about sex than they really are and hide what they don't know.

Finally, let your children know that you respect their ability to make their own decisions about these issues. The fear that your children will make the wrong decisions all too often turns into a self-fulfilling prophecy. The idea that you can control your children's sexual activity is an illusion. Demonstrating your faith in their ability to make decisions regarding sex—and providing them with all the information they need to make those decisions—help keep the lines of communication open between you. It also makes sexual acting out less attractive as a way to rebel when they reach adolescence.

Developing Empathy

A three-year-old who cries out, "Mommy! Look how big that man's nose is!" will probably be politely shushed by his mother and ignored by the man. An adult who makes an equivalent statement, however, might find his own nose swollen and hurting within seconds. The difference is much more than a matter of social graces. We do not expect three-year-olds to understand how the things they say affect other people's emotions. They are not empathic in the way adults or even well-adjusted six-year-olds are.

To empathize with someone is to understand what he is feeling or, more properly, to understand what *you* would feel like if you were in his situation. It is an extension of self-concept, but it is far more complex. It requires an awareness that others think of themselves in ways that are both similar to and different from the way you do and that they also have emotions that they associate with those thoughts and images.

Unlike intelligence and physical attractiveness, which depend largely on genetics, empathy is a skill children learn. Its value is multifold. Children who are empathic tend to do better in school, in social situations, and in their adult careers. Children and teenagers who have the greatest amount of skill at empathy are viewed as leaders by their peers. The best teachers of that skill are the children's parents.

The precursors of empathy can be seen in children within the first day or two of life. A crying newborn child in a hospital nursery will often trigger crying among other infants in the room. Such crying is not a true display of empathy. The newborn infant appears to be simply responding to a sound that makes him uncomfortable, much as he would to any loud noise.

Toddlers sometimes show behavior closer to true empathy in their first efforts to connect another person's discomfort with their own. When a two-year-old sees his mother crying, he may also become upset and offer her a toy he's been playing with or a cookie he's been nibbling. He is giving his mother something that he knows has made him feel better when he has cried. It is unclear, however, whether the child understands what his mother is feeling or is simply upset by the way she is acting, much in the way a puppy will come up and lick the face of someone who's crying.

By the time a child is about four years old, he begins to associate his emotions with the feelings of others. While one child says he has a stomachache, some four-year-olds may come over and comfort him. Others, much to the bewilderment and disappointment of parents and teachers, will walk over to the child and punch him in the stomach. Yet in each case the healthy child is demonstrating his empathy for the one who is ill. The aggressive child does not know what to do with the skill he's been developing. The other child's discomfort makes him feel uncomfortable. Instead of running away or rubbing his own stomach, as he might have done a year earlier, he feels frustrated and lashes out.

Teaching Empathy

Although the best training for empathy begins in infancy, it's never too late to start. Infants and toddlers learn the most by how their parents treat them when they are cranky, frightened, or upset. By the time a child is in preschool class, you can begin talking about how other people feel.

The way you show your own empathy, however, may be more important than anything you say. If your three-year-old cries out, "Look at the fat lady!" and you publicly bawl out your child and say that he shouldn't embarrass other people, you're working against yourself. Instead, quietly and gently explain why saying that may make the woman feel bad. Ask him if he's ever felt bad because of something a person said. Even so, some three-year-olds may be too young to comprehend what you are saying.

When a child is about five, he can learn about empathy by talking about hypothetical problems. How would you feel if someone took a toy away from you? How would your friend feel if someone took a toy away from him? By the time a child is eight he can grapple with more complex moral decisions in which he must realize that someone else's feelings may be different from his own.

Children's Perceptions of Disabilities

One of the most difficult tests of empathy occurs when children are faced with another child's disability. Children view disabilities and disfigurements in different ways from adults. Their questions and fears, as well as the facets to which they pay little attention, tell us about issues that concern them about themselves. Helping able-bodied children understand what has happened to someone who is sick, scarred, or disabled may be complex and often may run contrary to our intuitions.

While toddlers usually pay little attention to physical differences in their playmates, preschoolers begin to make judgments on how other children act and look. They don't think of disabilities as something that could happen to them. Instead, they associate differences in appearance with differences in personality and virtue, much the way that children's books seldom show pretty witches and ugly princes.

The responses of slightly older children to people who are disabled, disfigured, or ill reflect the ways they are trying to make sense of the world. Eight-year-olds, for example, are notorious collectors of everything from rocks to bugs to dolls. They spend hours arranging and rearranging their collections, for they have made the powerful discovery that things fall into patterns and categories. That's why a third grader who has a classmate with cancer will often ask for specific information about the disease or its treatment that makes adults uncomfortable. He may ask, "What color was the tumor? What did it feel like? What did they do with it when they cut it out?" All these questions reflect his way of figuring out where all this fits in the world.

Despite their extra years of practice with empathy, teenagers have a great deal of difficulty feeling comfortable around class-mates who have disabilities or who are in other ways different. There are several reasons for this apparent insensitivity and intolerance. Peer pressure is at its peak, as is the desire to fit in with the group, both of which conflict with their developing sense of empathy. Also, teenagers are going through some-times disturbing physical changes of their own. Seeing someone who has a physical disability or who, for example, has obvious scars from severe burns may be particularly threatening.

More than younger children, teenagers are scared that this sort of thing might happen to them. They are brimming with unasked and unanswered questions. How does it affect the other person's sexuality? Did the person develop the problem by doing something bad? Will they be rejected by their friends if they pay attention to this person?

Parents can sometimes diffuse their children's anxiety by bringing these unspoken questions to the surface. More impor-tant than knowing all the answers is showing teenagers that you won't be embarrassed by or think any less of them for having these concerns.

Learning Empathy for Someone Who's Different

Ever since federal legislation in the 1970's required, in effect, that handicapped children be included in public school classes with nonhandicapped children—a process popularly known as mainstreaming—the number of chil-dren with physical, emotional, and learning disabilities in traditional schools has significantly increased. So have the numbers of children with illnesses like cancer and AIDS and those disfigured by severe scarring from burns. The odds are greater than ever that a "normal" child will be in a classroom with someone who is profoundly "different."

Grade school children often react strongly and with ap-parent cruelty to someone who looks or acts in any way abnormal. They are likely, for example, to describe a classmate who is undergoing chemotherapy for cancer by saying, "He's bald, and he looks really ugly."

Many well-intentioned parents respond to such an insensitive comment by telling their child, "You shouldn't say he's ugly." Unfortunately, that emphasis on politeness and passing of judgment puts an immediate end to the discussion while giving a mixed message to the child. What was wrong: her perceptions, her interpretations, or simply speaking her thoughts out loud? How can she ask any more profound questions if her straightforward observations are met with an immediate rebuke?

Instead, ask your child, "Why do you think he's ugly?" By talking about the emotions behind the statement, you can help your child identify her real fears. Do the scars scare her? Is she frightened by how the other children treat this person? Is she afraid that this might happen to her? It may take a few conversations or even a few days for children to answer these questions and to ask questions of their own.

CHAPTER 5

Early Education

School, which in its broad definition includes any structured child care or teaching activities, quickly becomes the center of children's lives. All children's care givers—even those who care for infants—are educators as well. Although some parents wait until their children are old enough for kindergarten or the first grade, growing numbers of children find themselves in some form of organized child care within several months to a year or two after birth. Such early education appears to be highly influential in the way children later tackle the far more complex social and academic challenges of grade school and beyond.

It is a mistake to view these early child care experiences as little more than baby-sitting. It is equally wrong, however, to assume that a high price charged by a large private center guarantees better child care than is available in a community-based program or a family day care home. Evaluating the quality of such services requires, in addition to an adult's perspective, the ability to think and see things like a child and to understand the different developmental tasks that children face as infants, toddlers, and preschoolers.

Without this ability to understand the minds of children and to view things as they do, some of the approaches and techniques used by good early childhood educators will appear to make little sense. Equally important, understanding the needs and capabilities of children at different developmental stages will help prevent you from wasting your time and money on those few programs that appeal to the vanities of parents instead of the needs of children.

Choosing a person or institution to care for their young children is one of the most stressful decisions parents make. That stress is both philosophical and practical. Almost all parents believe, probably correctly, that they can care for their children better than outsiders can. Also, the odds are fairly high that the mothers of today's parents cared for them at home until they were old enough for school. Looking for a child care program—especially an infant care program—can engender feelings of guilt.

Yet the decisions our parents made a generation ago are often impractical today. The growing number of single parents simply do not have the option not to work. Many families need two paychecks to survive and cannot afford to have one parent at home during the day. Other parents, who may be able to do very well on only one source of income, may want to continue their careers with as little interruption as possible. They enjoy their work and feel that they would be resentful of their children if they were to stay home. In each case, the decision to look for outside child care is not made lightly.

Day Care Versus Child Care

The day care situation in the United States is a mess. For too many families day care costs too much money for services of marginal quality provided by well-intentioned but poorly trained, poorly paid, overworked workers. Symbolic of the problem is the name itself. This is more than a matter of petty semantics, for it reflects the emphasis of many centers. What we want is child care—a nurturing environment that focuses on the needs of children. What we all too often get is day care—a place where children can pass the time while their parents are working. The priority is filling time for the babies and toddlers and providing much needed time for the working parents. It is taking care of our days rather than taking care of our children.

A well-designed child care program can foster your child's emotional and physical development in ways you may not be able to do at home. Numerous studies have shown that children who attend high-quality group day care may be more self-confident and relate better to both children and adults than children who stay at home. A poor program, however, can be little more than a preschool parking lot. Unfortunately few parents know how to look for the subtle signs that help distinguish between a poor program and an excellent one. Asking about a license and comparing fees with other centers may not give them the information they need. Yet parents cannot afford to wait for their children to tell them through their words or their actions if they are old enough to do so, that there are problems with their care.

Looking for child care is an emotional as well as a logical process. Because infants and toddlers are so vulnerable, we respond to stories about communicable diseases, sexual abuse, or fires at child care programs with outrage and, as we look for care for our own children, with fear. A day care worker, more than any other teacher, must be a substitute parent.

Child care is a booming industry. There were more than 60,000 licensed day care centers in this country in the late 1980's. Most of these centers are operated as independent or franchised businesses, by community groups such as YWCAs or by churches. At that same time there were also more than 161,000 licensed family day care homes, where groups of up to about a dozen children receive care. Despite these impressive numbers, most children receive care from a third type of child care provider: an unlicensed family day care home.

The assurances given by a day care license vary dramatically from state to state. Some have strict requirements that involve on-site inspections for health care, fire safety, sanitation, and other possible problems. In other states a license may not mean anything since it is issued to almost anyone who fills out an application and pays a fee to register a family day care home. The minimum ratio of adults to infants or toddlers also changes in different parts of the country and may even change between counties within a particular state. This ratio, which ranges from one adult for every four infants to one adult for every eight infants, is especially critical since infants require more individual care than older children.

Unlicensed family programs, which can operate legally out of a home, do not have to meet any of those requirements. This does not mean, however, that family child care is of lower quality than child care at a licensed center. In fact, very good unlicensed family care may be more advantageous for a very young child because of its homelike atmosphere. It's also good for older children who attend a day care program after school and who do well in a less structured environment.

Nor do the high fees charged by some programs guarantee that they provide better child care than less expensive programs. Although family child care homes usually charge less than child care centers, fees can range from a few hundred dollars a month for a government-subsidized program for low-income families to tuitions that rival the cost of sending a child to an Ivy League college. Harvard, of course, does not provide daily snacks as part of its package.

Evaluating Child Care

How, then, do you evaluate the quality of a program and the people who run it? Your approach to evaluating either a child care center or a family child care home should be the same. First, talk to the center director or family child care provider on the phone to see if there are any openings. Ask about dropping by to visit the program. If the provider immediately discourages visiting or is at all negative, don't bother going. It's probably a sign of problems—anything from understaffing to neglect or abuse of the children. A good program welcomes visitors at all times.

Visit during the morning when children are the most active. (If you visit after lunch, most of the children will be asleep.) Your stay should last at least an hour. First, look at how safe the rooms are:

- Do electrical outlets have safety caps?
- Are there bars or gates on windows above the first floor?
- Are there gates to prevent babies and toddlers from falling down stairs?
- Are there devices on the doorknobs that make it difficult for toddlers to enter a room where they don't belong?
- Is the number of the local poison control center prominently posted near the telephone?
- Is there more than one exit in case there is a fire?
- None of the care givers should be smoking.

Notice if the decorations in the room are designed for the children.

- Is there a mirror or colorful picture next to the changing table in the infant room?
- Is the children's artwork hung at their eye level? For toddlers that may mean it's only a foot or so off the floor.
- Is the children's artwork recent, or are there still Christmas pictures up in February?
- Can the children see reminders of home such as photographs of their parents?

The quality and interest of the care givers are much more important than the program's facilities:

- The people caring for infants should talk to them while changing or dressing them.
- There should be at least one adult in the room for every four infants.
- An infant room that smells of either soiled diapers or strong disinfectant may have a larger sanitation problem.

Watch how the care givers interact with the toddlers and preschoolers. They should be spending most of their time on their knees or sitting down with small groups of children. A good program will combine individual activities chosen by the children with group activities chosen by the adult.

One way to distinguish between a program that's attuned to the development of your child and a program that's mostly custodial is to watch what the care givers do when the children are outdoors. Care givers in a developmental program will continue to guide and play with the children. A custodial program will use the time outside simply to let the children burn off energy.

How do the adults respond to routine crises, such as fights between children or a child who is crying? What do they do with a child who's destructive? How do they handle a child who soils his pants? The care giver should show respect for the child's emotions rather than simply say that he shouldn't be doing that. Beware of care givers who shame a child.

Next, talk to the director or family day care provider. She will probably give you information about fees, sick child policies, food, and hours—the questions most parents ask. Find out about the qualifications of the staff. Look for specific training in child development rather than general statements about a college degree. Get the names and phone numbers of three or four parents who have children in the program. If she's a family day care provider, find out what will happen if she's sick or takes a vacation.

Ask her what she does to prevent sexual or physical abuse of the children in her program. She should feel comfortable talking about it. Find out what types of background checks she does on her employees, including janitors and kitchen help. What would she do if someone new came to pick up your child at the end of the day?

Before you leave, take another look in the main room at the number of care givers. Most of the money you pay in tuition should be going toward staff costs. The program that invests money in people is putting its money in the right place.

Preschool and Kindergarten

Satirist Dave Barry, his tongue planted firmly in his cheek, recommends that parents select a preschool with a strong pre-business curriculum that emphasizes blocks rather than a liberal arts curriculum that emphasizes gerbils. His quip reflects both the increased diversity of programs available to very young children and the growing concern among parents that choosing the wrong early-childhood-education program will put their children at a competitive disadvantage, not just in elementary school but in adult life.

Although Mr. Barry has purposely carried the concept to extremes, many parents searching for a preschool or a kindergarten wonder how much emphasis should be put on traditional academic skills, such as arithmetic or reading preparation. Early-childhood-education experts have found that preschools that try to put children on the fast track by mimicking elementary schools may be doing more harm than good.

There are no shortcuts to genius. Before a child learns a skill, such as reading or writing or playing the piano, he or she has to have the intellectual abilities—what psychologists call cognitive development—and the physical coordination necessary to accomplish the task. Beware of programs that promise to turn your child into a budding Einstein or that purport to give children lifelong advantages by teaching them sophisticated material at a very young age. Showing a six-month-old child slides of Renaissance art of Western Europe will benefit only the person who made a profit by selling you the slides.

Creating a Musician

I knew a music theory professor at a major conservatory who understood just enough about psychology to get into trouble. During his wife's pregnancy he remembered that food is a tremendously powerful reinforcer. When people or animals associate something with food, he vaguely recalled from his introductory psychology course, they tend to like it. At least it was something like that.

He also knew about the Suzuki method of training very young children to be musicians. In essence, Suzuki music teachers have children play the same piece of music over and over and over again.

Armed with this information, he decided that he and his wife would turn their child into a musical prodigy by combining those two powerful tools. He could do this, he figured, by playing music every time his child was being breast-fed. He would condition the child to like music by pairing it with food. Not only that, but while the child was nursing, the father would employ the Suzuki technique of playing only one piece of music. He and his wife chose the first movement of Bach's Third Brandenburg Concerto. Armed with his trusty cassette recorder, he went off to make psychological history.

By the end of three months everything seemed to be going well. Both parents were thoroughly bored with the Third Brandenburg by now, of course, since they were listening to it every three or four hours, day and night. But they kept it up, congratulating themselves on how well their child was thriving and waiting with eager anticipation to see whether they were cultivating a composer, a conductor, or a performer.

One night, as he crawled into bed next to his wife, the music theory professor turned on the clock radio on the bedstand. There it was: the Third Brandenburg Concerto. Quickly he turned to his wife to get her reaction and then started laughing at himself because of what he saw. At the sound of the music, milk had started pouring from his wife's breasts. She, not their child, was the one who had been conditioned to respond to the music.

Some preschools, perhaps in response to the "back to basics" movement or a misunderstanding of some overseas school systems, such as those in Japan, are trying to give young children a head start on their peers by offering formal classes in foreign languages or mathematics. At first blush, pushing early academics by structuring nursery school and kindergarten as if they were junior versions of grade school, complete with workbooks and formal classes, may appear to make sense. A child who has memorized basic sums and who can recognize the letters of the alphabet at age four would, through simple logic, seem to have a leg up on less knowledgeable students who are struggling with those tasks in the first grade. The realities, unfortunately, are different. Pushing early academics appears at best to be worthless and at worst to turn some young children's perception of school from an exciting place to a place filled with stress and failure.

The biggest problem with bringing the techniques of elementary and high school educations down into the very early years is that the precursors to later academic skills, according to research in early childhood education, are often different from what many parents think. Simply memorizing letters doesn't necessarily help a preschooler learn to read later on. The precursors of reading are having stories read to you, making up stories, and seeing labels on objects so that you can make the connection between a printed word and the object itself.

The same can be said for mathematics. Rote memorization of numbers or addition facts are often less valuable than spending time playing with blocks. One of the major tasks facing preschool children is mastery of the very complex concept that abstract symbols can relate to objects in the real world. It is a concept to which adults hardly give a second thought. Preschoolers must learn that although the word "banana" can represent or symbolize a particular fruit, the word itself is not a banana and cannot be eaten. Similarly, five is a larger number than two even when the five refers to a number of strawberries and the two refers to a number of elephants or when the symbol "5" is an inch tall and the symbol "2" is a foot tall.

Only when this concept is understood do letters and numbers begin to make sense. Giving preschoolers words to memorize or sums to calculate before they master that concept is, according to early-childhood-education research, a waste of time. The four-year-old child who is sitting at a desk with a workbook in front of him is not being well served. In fact, teaching children symbols before they know what those symbols stand for or how they operate may make things more difficult for them in later years. Such a superficial understanding is like building the second floor of a house before you've built the foundation. The children who have simply memorized a bunch of facts have no sense of mastery over the material. All too often that type of early introduction to traditional academics leaves children feeling flustered and incompetent rather than masterful.

The most critical lesson in kindergarten or preschool is not directly related to the amount of "content" children can recall on cue. Instead, it is the realization that they can be effective and successful learners. Early education has succeeded when children have learned to feel good about themselves.

What to Look for in a Preschool

There are several guidelines for selecting a good preschool or kindergarten. Safety issues are similar to those for child care centers:

- Are there smoke detectors in every room?
- Are toxic materials such as cleaning fluids stored in locked cabinets?
- Are there cushioning materials such as wood chips under all areas where children climb or swing?
- Are emergency numbers posted conspicuously by telephones?

As with child care centers, preschools and kindergartens should welcome visitors at any time. A school that does not is not worth considering.

The classrooms should convey an air of excitement without mayhem, orderliness without regimentation. Children should know what's expected of them as soon as they walk through the door. That includes taking off their coats (with the help of the teacher, if needed) and properly storing them as well as anything else they've brought.

Speak with the teachers about how the school day is structured. Children should have some control over which activities they'll participate in. Stay away from preschools where the teacher is choosing everything that the child is going to be doing throughout the day.

Look at the ratio of teachers to students. The National Association for the Education of Young Children recommends no fewer than one teacher and one assistant for every group of up to sixteen three-year-olds or twenty-two four- or five-year-olds. As with evaluating care for infants and toddlers, ask about the teachers' and assistants' specific training in early education. In the long run the educational philosophy of the school is frequently less important than the individual teachers' attitudes toward children.

Finally, look at how the children interact with their teachers and with one another. One of the goals of early education is to teach children how to deal with other people in a variety of situations. The school should set a tone of civility. There should be fun, laughing, and excitement, but there shouldn't be chaos.

Repeating an Early Grade in School

A generation or two ago it was common for children who were doing poorly in school to be given a "social promotion" to the next grade. Having a child repeat a grade was often viewed as a black mark against the teacher and the school. It was an admission that the adults in the school system had somehow failed. The folly of this approach, especially in junior high and high schools, became apparent as an embarrassing number of high school graduates were unable to read simple texts, add columns of numbers, or fill out employment applications. The children had passed, but the system had failed.

Part of the reaction to that travesty was the back to basics movement and, later, the introduction of mandatory entrance examinations for some first-grade classes. Educators wanted to be able to pick out as early as possible those children who were having trouble in school. If tutoring or other special programs didn't help, the next step would be simply to have the child repeat the grade. It appeared to be the fairest and most appropriate way to handle the situation. But studies comparing children who were retained in an early grade and children with similar academic performance who were promoted show that the issue is not clear-cut.

This is especially true during the first year or two of school. Both parents and children invest a great deal emotionally in that introduction to academia. To struggle and to fail so close to the starting line are especially painful. Yet there is something special about those first years of school that many, if not most, parents (and quite a few teachers) fail to realize. We can see a strong pattern to both success and frustration among children in early education. To understand that pattern and the ways we should begin understanding children's successes and failures in kindergarten and the first two grades, we need to do a bit of arithmetic.

Early success in school appears to be largely a matter of ratios. No parent would expect even the brightest 6-month-old child to be able to accomplish the same tasks as a typical 12-month-old child. The older child has had twice the amount of time to work on the skills needed to live and learn. Similarly, few parents would expect to see much difference in academic performance between a child who's 17 years old (204 months, in case you've given up counting) and one who's 17½ years old (210 months). Despite the same 6-month gap in age, the ratio has shifted from 12:6 (2.00) to 210:204 (1.03). Although we may cavalierly say that we pay little attention to the difference between the two teenagers because they're so close in age, what we're really looking at is that ratio rather than the absolute difference.

In general, success in kindergarten is correlated with a child's age. Older children do better than younger children regardless of how intelligent they are. The same holds true on standardized tests of achievement given to first graders. That age-related difference disappears, say education researchers, by the third grade.

What this means is that when September rolls around and children begin kindergarten, a five-and-one-half-year-old has a significant advantage over a five-year-old, regardless of sex, socioeconomic status, or IQ score (at least within reason). That ratio of 66 months to 60 months (1.10) is still significantly high enough to influence the two children's relative abilities to cope with the material covered in kindergarten. This doesn't mean that *all* five-and-one-half-year-old children will do better than *all* five-year-old children, but if you were to place a bet on which kids will do well and which will do poorly during their first few years of school, the first thing you should look at is their ages.

By the time the same children reach the third grade (96 months and 102 months) the ratio of ages has dropped to 1.06 and is apparently close enough to 1.00 to be of little practical consequence. In fact, studies of children who appear to be having academic problems in kindergarten and the first grade show that a very large proportion of them have caught up with their peers by the third grade, especially if they have been given remedial help.

At the same time the emotional consequences of being retained in an early grade appear to be more significant than educators and psychologists previously thought. Children who repeat kindergarten report thinking of themselves as failures, feeling that they don't fit in with the new children, and being teased about the retention. This combination of lack of apparent academic benefit with pervasive emotional consequences to those children who are not promoted has led the National Association of School Psychologists to issue a position statement in 1988 encouraging educators and psychologists to look for alternatives to having a very young child repeat a grade.

> A review of the research on the effectiveness of retention of students shows disparity between best practice and actual practice. . . .
> Furthermore, more positive alternatives to retention may exist that will have a far greater likelihood of success. Given the lack of convincing evidence supporting the use of retention, it is imperative that school psychologists and educators give careful consideration to other options and alternatives that will better meet the needs of low-achieving students. Alternative instructional strategies . . . have all been shown to result in achievement and/or self-concept gains for low achievers. . . .
> The research reviewed in this supporting document reveals that retention is a costly and largely ineffective way to deal with academic failure. . . . Neither social promotion nor retention is the answer to pressing needs in the schools. . . . Our children demand alternatives which address their needs effectively and do not penalize them for academic failure.*

This is not to say that having a child repeat a grade is never the right thing to do. It should, however, be a last resort, *espe-*

* Mary Ann Rafoth, Peg Dawson, and Karen Carey, "NASP Supporting Paper on Student Retention," National Association of School Psychologists, December 1988.

cially in kindergarten or the first few years of grade school. (It is far better, if a child is either significantly younger than his or her prospective kindergarten classmates or less emotionally mature than they are, to delay entry into kindergarten by a year. This will make the child one of the oldest in the class instead of one of the youngest and will greatly increase the odds of that child's success.) Remember that to a child, repeating a grade is like eating a reheated dinner. It seldom tastes nearly as good the second time around.

If Your Child Is Having Trouble in Kindergarten

There are several things you can do if your child's kindergarten teachers recommend retention:

• First, ask your child what he or she thinks. If the child wants to go on, that's very important. A few children recognize that they're not ready for the first grade and will say that they want to stay in kindergarten for another year. In general, however, if children aren't significantly younger than their classmates and if they don't have serious emotional or intellectual problems, it's usually a good idea to encourage promotion rather than retention.

• Ask why the teachers think your child needs more time to develop instead of extra help during the summer or in the first grade. Find out the ways in which the proposed second year of kindergarten will be different from the current year. If it's simply a repetition, your child will likely become bored and frustrated.

• Explore alternative forms of help for your child, both in school and at home. Are there things that you could do, such as labeling drawers or reading more stories aloud, that will help your child catch up?

• Remember that most children who are having trouble in kindergarten catch up with their peers within a few years. Keep encouraging your child. In the long run, it doesn't matter whether your child learned to read at age five, six, or seven.

CHAPTER 6

The Art of Discipline

FEW THINGS strain the communication between parents and children more than ineffective attempts at discipline. Pediatricians receive calls from concerned mothers of toddlers who have suddenly started throwing tantrums whenever they don't get what they want. Fathers dread going on long car trips with their preschoolers because the children whine incessantly. Psychotherapists routinely are consulted by parents who complain that their children don't listen to them and don't do what they say. Often these children have similar complaints about their parents. In many cases, each side is misinterpreting the communications of the other and failing to understand the other's motivations, limits, and assumptions.

This frustration that surrounds this problem is not new. Dr. Irwin Hyman, a professor of school psychology at Temple University who specializes in issues related to discipline, recently wrote that archaeologists have uncovered six-thousand-year-old clay tablets from southern Babylonia that describe in great detail how the adults of that community found the younger generation to be insolent and disobedient. The solution they recommended, translated as best we can, was a swat on the behind.

Knowing that the problem of how and when to discipline children has been around for a while is of little help to parents who are angry and frustrated by their children's behavior. Even less useful are biblical warnings about sparing rods and spoiling children and more modern treatises claiming that stifling children's free expressions will somehow warp their psyches. Child-rearing theory usually goes out the window when your preschooler decides to improve the colors of a Persian rug with finger paints or your ten-year-old's verbal taunts have reduced his younger sister to tears. There comes a time when even the most educated and sensitive parent says, "To hell with psychology. I've had enough!"

What usually follows such episodes is not discipline but punishment. The two are often confused since, to many people, the term "discipline" conjures up images of Marine Corps drill instructors ordering their cowering recruits to do extra push-ups or of children being sent to their rooms without dessert. Punishment involves imposing a negative consequence to an unwanted behavior.

What Is Discipline?

Discipline is very different from punishment, as can be seen from one of its Latin roots, *discipulus,* which means "a learner." It shares that ancestry with the English word "disciple." At its core discipline involves teaching rather than punishment. The swat on the behind that the Babylonians prescribed, while well intended, was punishment rather than discipline. This is not to say that punishment is never appropriate. However, it seldom teaches the child anything, and when it does, it often teaches something different from what was intended. Hitting a child for misbehaving lets children know that it's all right for big people to control little people through physical violence.

The most effective forms of discipline—those approaches that teach children ways of behaving appropriately—take into account stages of development. Some behaviors are simply outside the abilities of young children. You can't expect a three-year-old to sit quietly through a baseball game, any more than you can expect that same child to drive a car. Preschoolers are naturally attracted to everything that goes on around them and are incapable of focusing on a single task for as long a time as an adult or even an older child. That's why a young child left alone in a supermarket is likely to run through it and touch as much of it as he can. Such behavior is not always rebellious or spiteful, as it might be in a much older child; it reflects the child's level of development. Trying to get a preschooler to stand calmly by your side during a long shopping trip is guaranteed to be both frustrating and fruitless.

The simplest form of discipline is what's known as environmental control. It's something parents do naturally with infants but sometimes forget with older children. If your four-year-old can't sit at a dinner table at home for more than ten minutes, you know you'll be in for trouble if you take him to a restaurant, where there will be even more distractions than at home. The best form of discipline in this case is not to take the child to the restaurant. (This choice may not always be available to you, of course.) In time, when your child can sit still longer, restaurants will be more appropriate. Meanwhile, by avoiding the entire situation, you've saved both of you a lot of anger and frustration.

Another deceptively simple approach is to make use of your child's developmental stage through distraction. One of the classic examples of this approach, and how it may be modified for children who are at different developmental stages, is the long automobile trip. Until they reach the age at which they can get drivers' licenses, children tend to be poor travelers. A major trip in the family car contains the two elements for which children probably have the lowest tolerance: confinement and boredom. It is a recipe for trouble.

It also provides an excellent environment for demonstrating how understanding a child's stage of development can help ward off lost tempers and hurt feelings. Even though the words are the same, a cry of "I'm bored" from a nine-year-old means something different from its meaning to a five-year-old or a thirteen-year-old. Knowing how those differences reflect the child's level of development will help you choose the most effective response.

Distraction is most commonly used on trips with grade school children. Children this age are mastering issues related to categorizing and classifying information. One sign of this is their pervasive interest in collecting everything from baseball cards and coins to comic books and stuffed animals. Car games, such as competing to be the first person in the car to spot fifteen items starting with a particular letter or looking for license plates from twenty-five different states, make use of that developmental stage and prevent boredom. That approach, however, won't work with younger children since they don't share the same interest in categories or with early adolescents since they've already mastered the process of categorization.

Younger children can usually be distracted by playing with their toys, especially if they receive something new after a few hours. The critical factor here is the novelty of the item, not its cost, where it came from, or whether it's perceived as a present. Preschoolers, and to a lesser extent school-age children, are attracted to anything that is new. That's one of the reasons truck stops and other roadside restaurants do a good business selling overpriced, brightly colored toys. Young children find them irresistible, and parents, who've just put up with two hours of listening to cries of "Are we there yet?," consider the high price a trade-off for a half hour of quiet. The way to make use of this developmental stage without paying exorbitant prices for what is sometimes dangerous junk is to invest in some inexpensive, safe distractions before you leave for the trip and to open them one at a time when you think your child needs something new to keep occupied.

Early adolescents are caught in a bind. They are more sophisticated than younger children but not as patient as adults. They also crave responsibility. Making a thirteen-year-old the "official navigator" on the trip feeds the hunger for responsibility. By planning the route ahead of time, the child claims emotional ownership of the trip. By telling the driver when to turn, she exercises control and power within her family. Navigating is the next best thing to driving since it's something a younger child can't do or at least can't do as well. The trip, instead of being a cue for boredom, becomes a stepping-stone to adulthood.

Using Time-out

Not all behavior problems may be avoided so neatly. What should you do when you feel you're about to lose control and do something you may later regret? Which types of discipline and punishment are most effective, and which are a waste of time and effort?

One of the most powerful tools for disciplining a misbehaving child is known as time-out. If, for example, a child is hitting other children, tell him that what he is doing is unacceptable behavior and that he must go to his room for five or ten minutes. Set a kitchen timer for the desired time so that he knows when the time-out is over. Explain to him that if he leaves his room early, the timer will be reset to the original time-out period. If he whines or complains, ignore him.

Although this type of response may seem trivial to adults, it's remarkably effective with children. Like environmental control, it immediately removes the child from the location of the trouble and the cues that may have triggered it. It makes use of a child's natural desire for attention. It helps the child learn that there are consequences to inappropriate behavior. It avoids giving the child the negative attention that comes with being spanked or yelled at. Since you're not telling the child what to do when he's in his room, it avoids a power struggle. Perhaps most important, it gives both the parent and the child an opportunity to calm down. This is especially critical if parents feel that they are about to lose control.

The responses that do not work, at least in the long term, usually occur when parents respond to their own feelings rather than think about what happened from the child's point of view. That's when most spanking and slapping take place. You probably see this all the time in the supermarket or in other areas where a young child is likely to become very excited. The child does something that irritates the parent, who swats him or her without a moment's thought, as if the child were an irritating mosquito. It is simply a way—and an inappropriate way at that—for the parent to ventilate anger. The child learns nothing.

Responses That Backfire

One of the major problems parents have with disciplining their children effectively is understanding what is normal behavior and what is not. With toddlers and young children, a lot of what we call misbehavior appears to be genetically programmed. The young child who constantly tugs at her mother's arm in the department store is not trying to be bad. More likely, she's having trouble coping with not being able to have all the things she wants immediately and not being able to explore all of the things that catch her eye.

Punishing a child for such behavior doesn't do any good since it's developmentally appropriate—and usually very adaptive—for young children to want things immediately and to want to explore. Distracting the child by giving her something to examine—a technique that takes advantage of her developmental stage instead of fighting it—is more likely to prevent a problem.

Recognizing the key issues in a child's stage of development can help prevent problems with older children as well. A seven-year-old who insists on eating a very sugary cereal or some other objectionable food for breakfast is often more interested in having some say in what she eats than in eating any particular item.

Arguing with her over the ostensible "content" of the disagreement will usually lead to an upset child and a frustrated parent. When such a battle appears imminent, you can usually avoid a head-on conflict by offering the child a choice between two or three cereals, any one of which is acceptable to the parent. That way the child gets to have some control over what she does and the family avoids a blowup.

Since parents are, for the first dozen or so years of their children's lives, so much bigger than they are, it's easy to overuse raw power to get your children to submit. Every parent does it occasionally. But if you say, "Do it because I said so!" too much, you induce fear and resentment. As soon as the child is no longer totally dependent on you and can live with the fact that you're angry with him, you may be in for some major battles in which your child uses the same approach toward you.

I recently received a mailing for a parent education course that promised to teach ways of having your child immediately respond to everything you say. The technique involved little more than thinly veiled bullying of children. It made the family structure analogous to a wolf pack in which there is one "top dog" that almost always gets its way.

What the developers of this program failed to understand was the natural history of the wolf pack. Eventually one of the younger wolves becomes large enough and strong enough to challenge the pack leader to a fight successfully. The old leader is either killed or so badly beaten that he submits to the new leader and gives up all of his status. Frankly, it's not the way to run a family.

Losing your temper with your child may lead to reactions that parents often regret and may actually foster the cycle of misbehavior. A colleague told me of one school-age child whose parents had taken the child to a psychiatrist's office because of constant behavior problems. Recently the child had told them, "There's no way you can punish me to make me change."

The first thing the parents had to do was admit that their child was winning the power struggle. Their yelling and screaming had become rewards instead of punishments. Doing something bad was a predictable way of getting the parents' attention. Once they realized that what they had assumed was emotionally painful was, instead, rewarding, the solution became apparent.

Instead of yelling at their child when he was bad and generally ignoring him when he was good, they tried a new approach: They ignored his bad behavior and paid extra attention to him when he did something good. Although the approach was simple, the habits were hard to break. After a short period in which the child tried to get a rise out of his parents, he stopped behaving badly because he no longer got anything out of it. He had learned something. The discipline had worked where the punishment had not.

Temper Tantrums

The young child's eyes narrowed, and his skin became flushed until he took on the appearance of a three-foot-tall Genghis Khan. Then came the widemouthed scream—a cry that combined defiance, frustration, and the decibel level of an oversize boom box. He was a little more than three years old, and he was throwing a tantrum in the check-out line of the supermarket.

Temper tantrums are among the most frustrating discipline problems for parents of young children. They need not be so, especially if parents remember the connection between discipline and teaching. The child learns a great deal from the way a parent responds to a tantrum. The key for parents is to understand and control that communication in ways that at the time may not seem obvious. The first step is to understand why children throw tantrums.

Most tantrums, especially kicking and screaming tantrums, occur when a child is between two and four years old. The child is frustrated by something but doesn't have many ways to handle that frustration. Lacking the verbal skills to argue or bargain, the child does what he or she can do: scream.

Tantrums, especially if they are few and far between, usually shouldn't worry parents. In fact, they are such a normal aspect of development that a child who never throws a tantrum may be indicating that there's cause for concern. It's unclear why some children are more prone to throwing tantrums than others. Even identical twins may differ—a sign that it's not a simple choice between nature and nurture and that a combination of genetic factors, family environment, and possibly even diet may play a role.

It's clear, however, that a tantrum is one way young children test how much control they have over their environment. Whether it gets to the point of being a battle between parent and child depends upon how the parent reacts. The most common and least adaptive reactions of parents to tantrums are anger, embarrassment, frustration, and concern over how passersby judge them as parents and as human beings. A college acquaintance of mine told me how his younger brother used temper tantrums to get his way. When his mother would come close to him during a tantrum in a public place, the young boy would cower and scream out, "No! No! Don't hit me!" The mother, of course, immediately retreated and, to save herself further embarrassment, gave the boy what he wanted. The child had developed a very creative and, for a short while, successful technique for getting what he wanted.

My friend's wife then described a situation a year earlier in which she and their three-year-old daughter went into a toy store to buy a present for another child. Before entering the store, she carefully explained to her daughter that they were going to buy just that one thing and then leave. The girl agreed, and the mother was satisfied that all would go well. As soon as the two of them entered the store, however, the stakes immediately changed and all bets were off. Toys were no longer an abstraction. Instead, they were all around the child, appealing to her natural possessiveness. She quickly grabbed a doll, said she wanted it, and refused to leave the store without it.

The mother refused to give in and asked her daughter to put the doll back. The response of the girl was predictable: She threw a tantrum on the spot, crying and screaming and attracting a lot of attention from the other shoppers. The mother, although initially embarrassed, let the girl cry a bit and then carried her outside, away from the stimulation of the toys.

There was nothing malicious in the girl's insistence on keeping one of the dolls. To a child that age, promising not to want anything in order to go into the toy store and then, once inside, asking for something is neither manipulative nor contradictory. They are two independent situations that, in order to be linked, require intellectual abilities beyond those of a three-year-old. Her mother's refusal to give her the doll ("buying" the doll is another concept that was beyond her) was confusing and frustrating. She expressed that confusion and frustration in the best way she could.

Just as the onset of tantrums marks a particular stage of development, so does the shift away from them. Most children stop having tantrums when their verbal skills improve. By the time children are six or seven years old, they should be practicing more sophisticated and effective ways of coping with frustration, such as negotiating.

Responding to a Tantrum

There are several techniques that parents can use to help children learn that temper tantrums are ineffective and to encourage them to develop other ways of dealing with frustration:

• Relax. Take a deep breath. As long as your child is physically safe, there's no need to rush in. In fact, waiting a few seconds can actually work to your advantage.

• Remember that the worst thing you can do is to give the child what he or she is screaming for. If you give in to the child's tantrum, you reinforce it, and the child will have more tantrums and will resort to tantrums more quickly.

• As soon as you've sized up the situation, take control of your child's environment. That usually means removing the child from the site of the tantrum. The move needn't be far—and often can't be, since your child may choose to throw a tantrum while you're pushing a half-filled shopping cart past the candy section of the supermarket. Picking the child up and moving only a few feet is effective since it demonstrates to the child that you are taking control.

• As best you can, ignore the tantrum without ignoring the child. That means not screaming back, as tempting as that may be at the time. Acknowledge to your child that he or she is upset, but be firm in your resolve. Don't try to reason with a child throwing a tantrum. Children need to learn that they can have some control over their lives but that this isn't the way to get it.

• Tell the child why he can't have what he wants. Give him some autonomy that's more appropriate, such as choosing some music to listen to at home or between playing with several toys he already owns. Just be sure that you're not bribing the child, or you'll be facing more tantrums.

• Don't worry about what the people around you think. Most adults have been in exactly the same situation with their own children. They're more likely to be empathizing with you than criticizing you.

Disciplining Other People's Children

"I wanted to strangle the kid!" a friend of mine exclaimed as he recalled the recent behavior of a visiting child at his daughter's sixth birthday party. My friend is a family therapist who is among the most patient and understanding people I know. Although he did not yield to his urges and in fact handled the situation very well, his anger and frustration highlight the difficulties that arise when adults have to discipline other people's children.

In retrospect, the birthday party incident should not have been a surprise. It began when one of the twenty children attending couldn't sit still during a magic show. He began elbowing the children on either side of him. Since the child's parents were not around, the host asked him to sit quietly. Five minutes later the child's elbows were flying again.

"I picked him up and took him away from the rest of the group," the host recalled. "I looked at him eyeball to eyeball and explained that his behavior was not permitted in our house. He agreed to behave properly."

Following the magic show, the children took turns trying to break open a piñata with a plastic baseball bat. When the misbehaving child's turn came, he grabbed the bat and started hitting the other children over the head. The host took away the bat and, keeping his own primitive responses in check, escorted the child to an adjacent room until they both calmed down.

Birthday parties are among the most likely situations to trigger aggressive behaviors among visiting children under the age of seven or eight. Children of that age have not yet developed a sense of empathy and, therefore, get little joy from someone else's celebration. They often feel ambivalent or jealous that another child is the center of attention and that they must give a gift without immediately receiving an equal or better gift in return. These feelings, when combined with the extra stimulation of ice cream, cake, entertainment, and party games, may become overwhelming. Faced with this situation, some children lose control. Their disruptive, acting-out behavior is contagious and rapidly spreads to other overstimulated children.

Such out-of-control behavior is much less common when young children are playing in small groups. Instead, parents are more likely to observe arguing, taunting, or teasing. Although such behavior may not be nice, unless it is dangerous, parents need not be as concerned or as quick to intervene. In fact, certain types of fighting between young children may serve a very useful purpose, for it can teach them ways of handling disagreements with others.

The places where children's disruptive behaviors occur may be more important than what those children do when they're out of control. Most emotionally healthy children are more constrained when they are at friends' houses than when they are at home. One reason is that children feel more secure in their relationships with their parents than in their relationships with other adults. They know that their parents will love them even if they do something bad. It's a sign of a more serious problem, however, when a child is controlled at home and uncontrolled at school or at other people's houses.

How and When to Discipline Someone Else's Child

Coping with other people's misbehaving young children is often more complex and emotionally draining than disciplining one's own. The fact that the child's actions are no reflection on your own skills as a parent is of little comfort at the time.

Certain unsafe behaviors, such as playing with sharp objects or running onto a road, require immediate reactions from all adults. But what about more benign areas, such as table manners or language? The child may come from a family that has different standards and expectations of behavior. The child's parents may interpret an outside adult's attempts at discipline as an affront to them or, at an extreme, as an assault upon their child. By permitting another child to behave in a way you do not approve, are you giving a mixed and confusing message to your own children? Here are some guidelines:

• Remember that you have the right to make the rules in your own house. Just because the other child insists that his parents allow him to do something doesn't mean you have to allow it as well. Also, with young children, don't worry about trying to justify your rules. They're not mature enough to understand logical thought. Instead, simply state the rules and repeat them when necessary.

• Remember that young children may not be aware of alternative behaviors that adults take for granted. Stating that talking at the dinner table with a mouthful of food is not acceptable may do little to change the behavior of a four-year-old unless the child is also told that he or she should swallow the food before speaking. Similarly, telling children that roughhousing indoors is not allowed will often have little effect unless you provide them with an alternative activity that also allows them to burn off energy.

• Large groups of children require different tactics. A visiting child who is out of control when he's part of a group will have a great deal of trouble regaining his composure unless he's physically removed from that setting. It's often useful to take the child to a different room and give the child something quiet to do, such as reading a book or listening to a tape. If that doesn't work, don't punish the child since he probably won't learn what you're hoping he will. Instead, call the parents and tell them that their child is having a hard time handling the activities.

CHAPTER 7

Behavior Problems

THE PRINCIPAL language of children is their behavior. There are times when that language is subtle yet eloquent, when the shades of meaning are lost on outsiders. A mother and father can quickly discern whether their infant's cry means he's hungry, tired, or simply lonely. Other adults hear no difference between the sounds. A teenager who dresses according to very different standards from her parents but whose clothing is nearly identical to what her friends wear is telling us her conflicting feelings over conformity. If you ask her what she's doing, she will probably tell you that she's rebelling against social pressure and expressing her individuality. But the similarity of her dress to that of her age-mates belies her claim of individual expression and clearly demonstrates her very powerful need to fit in with a social group.

There are times when a child's behavior is perplexing. Usually this is of no concern, for if an issue is large enough, a child will find many ways of expressing it, at least one of which will get through to the parent. Occasionally such behavior remains a frustrating mystery, especially when the child is doing something to which the parents object. This is where a parent's skill at decoding the nonverbal messages of a child becomes critical.

Children who cry or lie or repeatedly misbehave are trying to communicate something in the best way they know how. They may not have the verbal skills to express themselves clearly. Even if they are skilled at speech, they usually have neither the maturity nor the psychological insight to understand the causes of their anger, confusion, or pain. Much of the work of child psychologists and psychiatrists involves helping both parents and children understand the reasons for problem behaviors. Parents who hone their own skills at understanding a child's nonverbal language will find rearing children a less stressful experience.

A Different Perspective on Behavior Problems

Although it may not always feel like it at the time, part of the fun of being a parent is figuring out what's really going on when your child is behaving in ways you don't understand or approve and then coming up with ways of changing that behavior. The very complexity and challenge of the task are what makes it so rewarding when you've been successful. Doing this type of detective work well requires an awareness of the natural history of childhood, sophistication in the ways in which children act symbolically as well as directly, and, quite frankly, a good bit of luck. It also requires an awareness of your own biases and perspectives as an adult and as a parent, and recognition of how they differ from those of your children.

In some situations the behaviors that are so upsetting or worrisome are normal. Knowing that this is the case and that they will soon change relieves the burdens of guilt and anxiety you may be shouldering. Other times the problem behavior may be the only way the child can communicate his fears or other concerns. Interpreting it as malicious or spiteful when it is not makes things more difficult for everyone involved. There are also times when the problem you attribute to your child may be a reflection of your own unspoken or unexamined assumptions.

Finally, there are times when your child is simply being

cranky or bratty or manipulative. While these are also normal aspects of growing up, keep in mind that no amount of psychological sophistication is as beneficial to a cranky toddler as a one-hour nap. By the time your two-year-old gets cranky, you could probably use the break as well. Indulge yourself.

Why Hopping on Your Left Foot Will Make a Baby Stop Crying

Parents are always receiving inconsistent or even contradictory advice from other parents about solving the problems they have with their children. One of the best examples of this usually takes place a few weeks after the baby is born. The parents of a month-old baby are feeling frustrated and depressed as they listen to their apparently inconsolable child cry for several hours each day. Just as they have reached wits' end, one neighbor insists that singing to the child is the only solution, one set of in-laws suggests a colorful mobile, and another set of relatives recalls how two hours of rocking their children every night worked for them. Immediately the parents set about trying all these suggestions, yet the crying only gets worse. What's going on here? All of these techniques appeared to have worked on other children but not on theirs. Why?

Although a good deal of the variation in the amount of time an infant spends crying appears, according to some researchers and pediatricians, to be related to the infant's skills at self-calming—finding a way to retreat from the overstimulation of the outside world—that still does not explain why some parents swear by showing the child a stuffed animal and others describe the effectiveness of nightly rides in the car.

One evening the answer to this mystery came to me from an unlikely source. I remembered Myrtle, who had been one of the best psychology teachers I ever had. Myrtle had almost everything going for her. She was intelligent. She was beautiful. She also had white whiskers and a tail that was seven inches long. Myrtle, you see, was a gentle laboratory rat whose name was an acronym for May Your Rat Thus Learn Everything.

Although few of us, myself included, appreciate being compared with a laboratory rat, I'd like to make an exception for

Myrtle. In her own way she explained to me the reasons for some of the problems I'd occasionally had as a student and later had as a psychologist and a parent, for Myrtle taught me about the seductiveness of superstitious behavior.

When I was a college student, I took an introductory course in animal learning. My first task in the laboratory was to teach Myrtle to press a bar in a Skinner box. If she pressed the bar, she would get a drink of water. I knew it would be futile to try to explain the task to Myrtle, so I simply deprived her of water for a few hours so that she would be a thirsty and, therefore, motivated lab partner. Myrtle quickly learned where the water dipper was. The bar, however, was a different matter. No matter how hard I tried, I couldn't get her to sit on her haunches and press the bar with her forefeet the way the other rats in the room did. I wondered if Myrtle was learning-disabled. What would the other students think of me if my rat couldn't keep up with her peers? Would bringing in another rat as a tutor help? What about my plans for her future?

Myrtle was apparently as frustrated with me as I was with her. Being a fastidious creature, she turned her back to the bar, sat up, and began to groom herself. Unfortunately the wire bars on the floor of the cage were more slippery than she had anticipated. While trying to preen the fur on her chest, she lost her balance, toppled over backwards, and hit her head on the bar.

Whir. Click. Dip. Thunk. All of a sudden the dipper appeared with some fresh water. Myrtle was ecstatic. She'd figured out how the system worked. After swallowing the water, she got back into position facing away from the mechanism and flung herself backward until her head hit the bar again. Whir. Click. Dip. Thunk. Water!

I watched as this otherwise dignified animal awkwardly thrust her cranium at the bar in order to accomplish what the other rats in the lab were doing more efficiently, if less dramatically. Eventually she started flopping onto her back from anywhere in the cage and then running to the dipper to look for her water. But she hadn't hit the bar, so it wasn't there. After only a few unrewarded pratfalls she stopped her gymnastics.

Myrtle had fallen into the trap of superstitious behavior. She acted as if there were a connection between her actions (falling over backward) and getting the reward (a drink of water) when, in fact, there was none. Had she been able to talk (it was, after all, an introductory class for both of us), she probably would have told me that falling over backward *caused* the water to appear.

Although human parents are obviously more sophisticated and intelligent than laboratory rats, we sometimes make the same type of mistake with our children. Usually it's because we don't understand some of the signs of our children's development. We can see this in a common parental response to the patterns of crying among newborn infants.

A two-week-old infant cries an average of one and a half hours every day. This increases to approximately three hours per day when the child is about six weeks old. By the time children are twelve weeks old, their daily crying has decreased dramatically and averages less than one hour. This same basic pattern of crying is present among children from a wide range of cultures throughout the world. It appears to be wired into the nervous system of our species.

Some parents, especially mothers who are breast-feeding their babies, are upset when their three-week-olds cry more than they did the week before. They worry that it's their fault. So they try doing something different. The crying gets worse over the next week, so they once again change what they are doing. They repeat this cycle until, when the children are six weeks old, the parents are ready to do some screaming themselves.

At this point one of the parents tries something new, such as singing a particular song to the baby or buying a new mobile for the child to look at. It really doesn't matter what the new thing is. It could even be having the father hop up and down on his left foot every two hours on odd-numbered days. The parents notice that the baby isn't crying as much. They redouble their efforts. The mother is singing to the child at every opportunity. The father is contemplating writing a book on the benefits of left-foot hopping. The child's crying decreases even more. The parents are overjoyed. They have found the solution.

The reality of the situation, of course, is that the child would have increased and decreased his or her crying *no matter what the parents had done*. The singing, the mobile, and the hopping have nothing whatsoever to do with the child's behavior. Because they appeared at the same time, however, we assume that they are related.

Another example of how knowing the natural history of childhood can save parents a lot of worry and upset has to do with the timing of crying. In general, babies cry more during the evening than during the day. Parents who are away from their babies during the day and return after five o'clock will often hear from the child's caretaker what a delight the baby was that day and how little he or she cried. An hour later the child is in tears.

Naturally the parents assume that it's something they did or something about them that their baby doesn't like. Even worse, when one parent is working and the other parent is caring for the baby at home, each begins to suspect that the baby doesn't really like the one who isn't at home during the day. The baby is barely a month old, and already this parent has been judged and found lacking! But once again the timing of the baby's crying had nothing to do with the parents' behaviors. The two things just happened to occur at the same time.

So, before you assume that your child behaved in a particular way because of something you did, think of Myrtle. Her headache may prevent you from getting one yourself.

Lying

There's only one thing I remember clearly about my third-grade classmate Clive. One morning he didn't have his arithmetic homework ready. When our teacher asked him where it was, Clive didn't miss a beat. "My cat ate it," he replied. There is something so vivid in the image of a cat choosing to make a late-night snack of some addition problems that I stand in awe of it more than a quarter of a century later.

Lying is an amazingly complex and sophisticated act. Even doing it poorly requires an awareness of the past and the future, a sense of values, the idea that different behaviors result in different consequences, and the ability to imagine those consequences. We used to think that lying was so complex that it was uniquely human. Animal researchers have shown that some apes are intelligent and sophisticated enough to share our ability to dissemble; they will hide food from other apes.

Everyone lies. But telling a lie can be different for children—especially young children—from what it is for adults. To children under the age of four there is no clear boundary between their imaginations and the real world. Their wishes become their realities. When a preschooler tells you that his imaginary playmate was the one who spilled the milk or tracked the mud onto the living-room carpet, he truly believes it. There is no malice in such lies—merely wishful thinking.

Three-year-olds, for example, see the world in black-and-white terms. That forces them to use a simple syllogism: They have been told that they should be good. They want to believe that they are good. Spilling the strawberry jam on the family's dog is bad. Any child who did that, they figure, must be a bad child. Therefore, they weren't the ones who poured jam all over the sleeping cocker spaniel. Denying their culpability is neither malicious nor sneaky; it just reflects the unshaded terms in which preschoolers view the world.

We can also see this unclear boundary between reality and fantasy in the way young children love to be told stories. To a preschooler, the big bad wolf really can blow down the walls of the three little pigs' houses, and a family of bears really does live in a house, sleep in beds, and eat porridge. There's no symbolism involved at all. It makes perfect sense to a three-year-old that a bear would sleep in a bed and that three pigs would live in adjacent houses.

Children this age are learning to be creative with words and images. There is none of the self-judgment adults put on their work. Every one of them is an artist and an actor. They don't have to be "good" at painting to paint or at storytelling to make up a story. Their creativity is practically unbounded. Occasionally lying at that young age is simply one sign of that creativity.

The vivid imagination and difficulty distinguishing between reality and fantasy in preschoolers bring about a few problems as well. Scary or violent stories, movies and television programs can be extremely frightening to very young children, especially when the themes revolve around the separation from or death of a parent. Classic children's stories that contain these themes, such as "Dumbo" or "Bambi," can simultaneously terrify a three-year-old, amuse a six-year-old, bore a fourteen-year-old, and bring tears to the eyes of a parent, all because of their different stages of development.

Preschool children will tell you that lying is "bad" or "a sin" but, if pressed, won't be able to tell you why. They have yet to connect the word with the deed but are sophisticated enough to have picked up the idea that whatever lying is, they should not admit to doing it. If you ask a five-year-old, she will probably tell you, pointblank, that she doesn't lie.

By the time children are in elementary school they recognize the value of lies as tools. A nine-year-old who breaks a dish at home and tells you that it was his younger sister's fault doesn't really believe what he is saying, even though he hopes you do. He is aware of the probable unpleasant consequences of breaking a dish and is simply protecting himself.

The Girl Who Stole Lunches

We can't always assume that children bring the same ethical values to lying that adults do. They are, however, excellent at emulating our behaviors. There are times when a child's lying can be a reflection of a much larger problem facing someone else in the family. In such situations, focusing too much attention on the lying can cause you to miss the greater and much more important problems.

A seven-year-old girl was described by her teachers as a chronic liar and thief. She would steal her classmates' lunches. Even on the several occasions when she was caught red-handed, the girl vehemently denied having stolen the lunches.

The girl's mother, an overworked, overstressed single parent, was very busy with her career. She projected the image of having total control over her life, despite all the problems she faced both personally and professionally. Such control was an extremely important issue for the mother. She outwardly denied any and all problems.

The girl had learned from her mother that it was important to be doing the right thing at all times. Because she was a young child, she could not simply tell her mother or her teachers that she was feeling pressures at home and that she wanted more attention paid to her. Stealing her classmates' lunches—an action that would obviously result in her being caught and that symbolically reflected her jealousy of the nurturance those other children apparently received—was a way for her to get the attention she wanted. Lying about the thefts, even in the face of irrefutable evidence, was merely her reflection of her mother's coping style.

School-age children will often begin telling a different type of lie from those told by younger children. These new lies are related to an awareness of and desire for status among their peers. They may talk about how their older sisters know particular rock music stars or how their parents are going to be making movies. These lies, if they occur only occasionally, should be of little concern to parents. In some ways they are a throwback to the wishful thinking type of lie seen in younger children. This kind of bragging is a way for them to cope with a new set of social pressures.

The quality of lies changes as children grow older. By the end of elementary school a child should be aware of how lies can affect other people. We need a certain degree of truthfulness to make the world work. People count on the statements of others when making decisions of their own.

The lies of teenagers often reflect the developmental issues they are working through, such as autonomy. Normal lying entwines itself with other forms of rebellion. When you set a curfew of 10:00 P.M. and your son comes back at 11:00 P.M., he will swear that you said the curfew was 11:00. His histrionics usually have little to do with the curfew itself. He is demonstrating his need to be separate from you. Although annoying, it is usually nothing to worry about.

What to Do When a Child Lies

It's naive to believe that all lies are bad and that children should never lie. While lying should be strongly discouraged, the fact that a child feels the need to lie in a given situation is potentially very important information. To make the best use of that information, we have to view such lies from a larger perspective.

What types of lies are normal? How much lying is too much? What should you do if your child lies to you? Many of the answers to these questions depend upon the age of the child and the pattern of the child's lies. Here are some guidelines:

• Instead of thinking of lying simply as something the child is doing wrong, try to think of it as a solution to a problem the child is having. The preschooler who blames her imaginary companion does not have the intellectual ability to separate doing something bad from being someone bad. Lying is her only choice. The older child has much more of a choice but for some reason feels uncomfortable with or fears the alternatives.

• Look for patterns in the child's lying. Does the child lie only about school or friends or money? Does the child lie mostly to a particular parent or teacher? Often the pattern of the lies will tell you more about the underlying problem than the content of each individual lie.

• Help children understand the difference between your disliking what they did and disliking them as people. Young children especially may be fearful that something they do will cause you to reject them. Hugging a child by putting an arm around her shoulder while you talk about this may be very reassuring since it demonstrates your ability to love her at the same time as you discuss something she's done that you don't like.

• Give your children permission to tell the truth. This may sound a bit silly—after all, you've tried to get them to tell the truth for years—but it really is a powerful tool in dealing with a problem. If you believe that your child is lying about something important or if you're concerned about a developing pattern of lies, tell the child that you're pretty sure he's lying. Explain that you don't want him to lie to you and that people usually lie when they're worried and upset about something. Ask him what's bothering him. He may not tell you. In fact, in many cases he may not really know what's bothering him. Simply knowing that you're willing to listen to the truth, even when it involves a problem, is often very reassuring.

• Show your children alternatives to lying. Let them know that a vase broken by accident will not be treated in the same way as a vase broken on purpose. Talk about how, if they break another child's toy, they can sometimes make amends by giving the child one of their own toys. Children may have to test the waters by admitting small mistakes or problems before getting to the real issues. Give them enough time for such testing and an opportunity to find out if you are true to your word.

• Admit your own mistakes around your children. This is extremely important. Preschoolers very often regard adults—especially their parents and teachers—as godlike creatures who know everything and are incapable of doing wrong. By showing them that you can make mistakes and correct them, you will give your children more helpful information about coping with problems than will come from hours of lectures on why lying is bad.

• Most children are more likely to lie to their parents about problems than they are to their siblings. You should look closely into a situation where a child lies to a brother or sister about something significant such as getting into trouble at school since it is an indication that the child is probably very concerned about what is happening to him.

• Although lying is normal for all children, you should be concerned when lying becomes one of a child's most frequently used ways of handling stressful problems. The actual number of lies usually isn't as important as a noticeable increase in frequency. At this point a parent should seek professional help from a qualified therapist.

• Be concerned about and get professional help for a child who is scrupulously honest to the point of hardly ever lying. Lying is a skill that children should be developing through regular practice. A near-total aversion to lying in a child is a sign that there is probably something very stressful happening in the child's life.

• Finally, don't try to hold your children to a higher standard of behavior than you hold yourself. After all, how many lies do you tell each week?

Natural Consequences

The mother of a seventeen-year-old girl asked a question at the end of a speech I gave on adolescent development. She appeared to be a very caring parent who was concerned about her daughter's style of doing homework. It seemed that the girl did her most creative work late at night, between the hours of 11:00 P.M. and 2:00 A.M. She asked what she should do to get her daughter to work earlier in the evening.

"Is she completing her homework assignments?" I asked.

"Yes, she does very well at school."

"Is she getting enough sleep?"

"She seems to be. Sometimes she'll take a nap in the evening. She says she's most creative late at night."

"Then what's the problem?"

"I think she should be doing the work earlier in the evening."

"It sounds like you disagree with her approach."

"Yes. I just don't think it's right. It's a real problem for her."

Despite her good intentions, the mother was having difficulty separating her own feelings from her daughter's actions. The girl had apparently worked out a successful way to do her homework at a time of day when she could do her best work yet still get enough sleep. The daughter seemed happy. The mother, however, could not see the situation from her daughter's perspective and, therefore, assumed that the daughter must be upset.

"One other thing," the mother continued. "I'm tired of her leaving dirty clothes all around her room." There were nods and other signs of agreement from parents sitting in the room.

"What happens when she does that?"

"I pick them up and bring them to the laundry."

"What would happen if you didn't pick them up?"

"Oh, I couldn't just let them sit there. She'd have nothing clean to wear to school"

"She's seventeen years old. She knows that clothes need to be washed. Then again, why should she pick up her clothes if she knows you'll do it for her? Try to picture what would happen if she woke up one morning and discovered that she had two weeks' worth of dirty clothes scattered around her room and no clean clothes in her closet."

"But I couldn't let that happen," she said, showing the strong feelings of protectiveness she felt toward her daughter.

"Why not? She would see the natural consequences of her behavior and she wouldn't be in any danger. She's leaving home in less than a year. She certainly won't have anyone to clean her room and do her laundry at college."

Some of the other members of the audience were, by this time, seeing the pattern in the relationship between this woman and her teenager. Her acts of love and support were becoming tainted by feelings of resentment that interfered with her ability to communicate with her daughter.

"And another thing," said the woman. "I'm tired of having to wake her up in the morning to be sure she gets to school on time."

"Why are you waking her up?" asked a mother from the audience who wanted to help the woman see the pattern in her interactions with her daughter.

"So I'm sure she's not late to school."

"What would happen if she were late?" asked a father in the audience.

The discussion went on like this for several minutes as more parents became involved and shared similar experiences and feelings. The mother appeared to have quite a few complaints about her teenage daughter, all of which centered on the issue of control. She was extremely uncomfortable letting her child make mistakes and suffer the natural consequences of those mistakes. Even when her daughter came up with an ingenious and successful approach to tapping her creativity, the mother felt uncomfortable because she could not control it.

The intentions of the mother were admirable. She wanted to

help her daughter succeed and to protect the girl from what the mother viewed as unnecessary pain. The difficulty arose from the extremes to which she took her actions and her reluctance to let her daughter make mistakes—and to succeed by recovering from those mistakes. The daughter was feeling undermined; the mother was feeling resentful because her demonstrations of love were not being appreciated.

Rather than step aside and allow her daughter to fail occasionally—an act that would be *temporarily* painful to both of them—the mother chose to live with the chronic pain of conflicting emotions. She did not like to see her daughter's room littered with dirty clothes, but she resented cleaning up the mess. She did not like the thought that her daughter might be late for school, but she resented waking the girl up every morning. The acts of simply closing her daughter's door so that she would not have to look at the mess and of buying her daughter an alarm clock so that the girl could wake herself up were not good enough. She told me that she would still be aware of the clothes behind the door and she would still worry about her daughter getting to school on time.

Whose Problem Is It?

One of the most challenging tasks parents face as they watch their children grow is abdicating control over their lives. It is a necessary detachment, so much so that when you speak of a healthy middle-aged man who has lived all his life with his mother, the listener will usually and sometimes unfairly infer things about their relationship. She must be domineering. He must be a Milquetoast.

It is appropriate to control much of a seven-year-old's schedule. It is inappropriate and self-defeating to try to exercise that same control over a seventeen-year-old. Adolescents will, of their own accord, rebel against parental controls that are constraining. "Be home by midnight." "But nobody else has to leave that early! Why can't I come home at two o'clock like my friends?" The parents' attempts at control are obvious and direct.

There are other situations when parents' attempts at controlling their children are more subtle and may, in fact, be initially perceived by the children as liberating rather than constraining. They generate problems that are ironically born out of love, not anger or distrust. The mother who picks up her teenager's dirty clothes from his room is unknowingly fostering his dependence upon her. At the time it feels understandably good to both parties. The mother feels needed and useful. The child has one less thing to worry about. The same may be said for a father who knocks on his daughter's door every morning to make sure she's awake and ready for school.

These are also battles for control over the child's life. It is a way of fostering a kind of mutually acceptable helplessness on the part of the child. Each side clings to an elusive and illusory memory of a time when responsibilities were simpler and lines of authority were clear-cut. Neither person must grow. Everything usually goes well until one of two things happens: The parents become angry or the children are on their own.

College administrators regularly tell bittersweet stories of parents who feel threatened by their children's imminent adulthood and have great difficulty letting go during freshman year. Some parents place daily wake-up calls to the dormitory. Others ask for class schedules so that they can remind their children to study for exams. Their relationships are frozen in time.

None of the issues raised by the frustrated parent the evening of my speech was related to the child's safety. There's no question, for example, that you should not let a child who does not have a driver's license go out for a spin in the family car. These types of issues do not bring about ambivalent feelings. Rather, this parent's frustrations were centered on relatively benign issues that were more symbolic than dangerous.

So one of the questions that should be asked by a parent who feels resentful about doing something for an adolescent is "Whose problem is it?" If your fifteen-year-old daughter has a messy room, who will suffer if she can't find something that she's looking for? She will. If your thirteen-year-old son doesn't keep track of his soccer team's schedule, who will suffer if he misses a game? He will. If the twins make a late-night pizza and leave the dirty dishes and utensils scattered about the kitchen, who cleans it up in the morning?

Let's play out this last fantasy a bit so that the benefits of letting adolescents cope with these types of problems on their own become clear. Here's one of many possible scenarios: Your twin teenagers have left assorted pizza-encrusted plates and pans in the kitchen from last night's snack. They know it's their job to clean up their own mess in common areas. They wake up the next morning a few minutes later than usual. Rather than face the prospect of pizza sauce that, by that afternoon, will need to be removed with a hammer and chisel, they decide to clean the mess in the kitchen.

Now they're late for school. They walk into their first period history class midway through a lecture on the War of 1812. When the teacher asks why they are late, they give the details of cleaning up the leftover pizza. Their classmates laugh at them. They feel embarrassed. The teacher assigns them extra work.

What have they learned? First, their actions, such as not cleaning up their own mess at the most appropriate time, have consequences. Second, telling people the complete truth (such as the details of the burned-on pizza sauce) can sometimes work against you. They would have been better off simply saying that they had no excuse. Fifteen years from now they will probably not remember anything about the War of 1812 except possibly the date, but they will remember those two lessons. It will have been a school day well spent.

CHAPTER 8

School

SCHOOL IS the institution we most associate with childhood. Children spend more time at school than they do any other place outside home. The influence of schools on our children is pervasive. Yet much of what children learn in school has little to do with the content of the courses they take and may, in fact, be far more important than the answers to any of the questions that appear on exams.

School offers children a chance to establish themselves as competent individuals apart from their parents. It allows children to try on different roles in a social group, to test their skills at leadership and negotiation, and to experiment with new facets of their identities. School is also a world that largely belongs to children. Parents are outsiders in the classroom. For many children, going to school or preschool is the first time they have been a part of something that was primarily their own.

While the structure and challenges of school, as well as the coursework it provides, can be very beneficial to children, it can be frustrating for parents. All children will occasionally be secretive or monosyllabic about that aspect of their lives. ("What did you learn in school today?" "Nothing.") Yet the verbal and nonverbal messages our children share with us tell us a great deal not only about whether they're having trouble with algebra but also about how they are handling the transition to their next stage of development. Are they beginning to think abstractly? Are they learning to cooperate on tasks? How are they allocating their time when they have several things to do? Are they showing an interest in the opposite sex?

The gulf between parents and schools is far greater in this country than it should be. Although most parents may not remember the specific fears and humiliations they suffered as children, they still feel uncomfortable in school buildings or challenging the authority of the teachers. Teachers often send mixed messages to parents as well. They welcome and encourage parental involvement as long as the parents don't try to change things too much. Yet the value of parents' involvement in their children's schooling is immeasurable. It is the clearest way of letting your children know that you think what they do during the day is important.

Children learn and remember at least as much from the context of the classroom as from the content of the coursework. If you doubt that, think about how well you would do if today you retook all the final exams from your senior year of high school. Few of you would pass them all without studying. (I certainly couldn't.) It is the emotions of the classroom that leave the most lasting and important marks. Do your children view themselves as successes or failures? Are they being encouraged to be inquisitive or passive? Are they afraid to challenge authority and to question assumptions? Do they feel comfortable adapting to change? Are they easily discouraged if they cannot arrive at a solution to a problem? The answers to those questions will give you a better appraisal of their education than any list of courses, grades, or test scores.

Discussions between parents and children about school tend to be laden with emotions. Parents bring with them their own psychological baggage from their experiences as students. We set expectations for our children based in part upon our own successes and failures. Those expectations may or may not be appropriate. We may react too strongly or not strongly enough if our children are having difficulty with schoolwork or show problems on their report cards. We may forget what it's like to see school through the eyes of a growing child.

A Child's-eye View of School

School is the major arena in which children go forth to do battle until they reach adulthood. For some, it appears as dangerous and frightening as any field of war, for they see it as a jungle filled with enemies and booby traps. School is a place that makes no pretense of equality. A student cannot be promoted by a teacher on the basis of performance alone. Even the brightest and most successful students remain almost completely powerless until they have graduated.

Our memories of school are often highly selective, especially if we were successful as students. We quickly forget the humiliations and the gut-level fears that we no longer face in the outside world. Imagine how you, as an adult, would react to a job in which you might be tested at any time, were constantly being publicly compared with other employees, had to put up with a lot of meaningless bureaucracy, and had so little control over your life that you needed someone else's permission to use the bathroom.

To understand the stresses of school on children, we must mentally look at the buildings and the teachers from only a few feet off the ground instead of our usual adult height. That is a very difficult task, and it is worth bending down and actually doing occasionally. Even mundane situations to which we, as adults, would hardly give a second thought may have profound effects on children. Having to find a classroom by themselves, facing a book report for the first time, adjusting to having different teachers for different subjects, and talking in front of the class may hold their own terrors.

I remember hearing one child, who was about to graduate from the sixth grade and move on to a larger junior high school, admit his fear of that new environment in wonderfully symbolic terms. He had heard that in junior high school you get a locker. He was afraid that he would forget the combination. No amount of reassurance that he wouldn't forget the numbers or that the lock could always be opened by someone from the principal's office would have helped this child, for the imagery was more important than the content. He feared being given new tasks and not being able to succeed as well as he had in the past. He feared being embarrassed and not fitting in with the older children. He feared being laughed at. Focusing on the locker would have missed the point.

School is also a place for success that rewards those children who fit in and do well. It may be a source of attention, prestige, and pride for those who are good at academics. It may provide a social group for children who are too shy to seek one of their own. It may offer support to children who need someone to talk to about problems at home. It may supply a sense of perspective and be a source of help to worried parents.

Homework

I distinctly remember my first homework assignment. I was in kindergarten. The teacher asked everyone in the class to look outside that night and find out where the moon was. That evening my mother and I walked a block from where we lived, and with a little help from her, I found the answer to my teacher's question: The moon was in the sky.

School assignments are seldom as much fun as that introduction to astronomy. Many children regard homework as little more than a curse to be avoided, rushed through, forgotten, or put off. Book reports are mentioned for the first time the evening before they are due. Math problems compete with the radio for a child's attention. Homework and studying are among the most common causes of arguments between parents and their children. One national survey conducted by the U.S. Department of Education in 1982 found that most high school seniors spend more time per night watching television than they spend per week doing homework.

But the problems start well before the final year of high school. Teachers report that they don't give much homework because it simply doesn't get done. Also, children are receiving their first major homework assignments later than they did twenty years ago. Today most public schools give almost no homework until the fifth or sixth grade and no serious homework until junior high school. A review of the literature on the relationship between homework and school success conducted by Dr. Jane C. Conoley, a professor of psychology at the University of Nebraska and former president of the division of school psychology of the American Psychological Association, indicates that waiting that long to assign homework is a mistake. Children who do homework in earlier grades tend to do better in school than those who do not. Children who receive their first significant homework assignments in junior high are often overwhelmed by the amount of organization they need to accomplish the task.

One rule of thumb that's generally accepted by school psychologists like Dr. Conoley is that the amount of time children study every weekday should be no less than ten minutes times their grade level. Thus a first grader would spend ten minutes per day studying at home and a high school senior would spend at least two hours. Children should spend that time studying even if they don't have any homework that's due.

The parents' roles in all this vary with the age of the children. If your children are less than ten years old, you'll probably have to be very involved in the mechanics of studying: reminding them of their study time, checking their assignments, and sometimes even sitting with them to make sure they get started. This extent of involvement can be difficult for busy parents who are tired at the end of the day. It is, however, an investment with a large payoff since children who develop a routine for doing their homework are generally more successful at school than those who do not. With slightly older children, especially those already in the habit of doing homework, you may simply have to check if they've done the work and be available to answer questions.

Many parents wonder if they should ever do their children's homework for them. The answer to that is straightforward: No. After all, do you really need to repeat the third grade or relearn how to write a book report? Doing your children's homework is a bit like believing that they can get into shape by watching someone else exercise. If, however, your children really cannot do the homework they've been assigned, it's time for an immediate conference with their teachers to find out what's going on.

Help with Homework Problems

There are times when the standard advice issued to parents about homework—find a quiet, well-lit place for your child to study, and establish a time to start the work—simply isn't enough. What do you do if your child still rushes through, avoids, forgets, or refuses to do homework? Here are some tips:

• First, stop whatever approach you're using, even if it's what your parents used or what your friends have recommended. For many parents, that means not criticizing their children and warning them about future dire consequences. If a technique hasn't worked so far, it's not magically going to get better. Besides, your kids have probably stopped paying attention to you when you say those things. You'll have to try a new approach.

• Often, getting children to do homework requires the parents to take an autocratic position on the matter. Tell your kids that you're open to discussing how late they stay out or what they eat for dinner, but doing homework is not a negotiable item. This lets them know that homework is a top priority in your family. Remember to reward the changes in their behaviors, such as finishing assignments on time or studying for the designated amount of time, instead of their grades. If the behaviors change, the child's grades will probably improve.

• Remove the children's incentive for racing through homework in order to watch television or play by insisting that they spend the remaining time allocated for homework sitting at their desks studying or reading. With some families it's very useful to declare the house a "TV-free zone" from Mondays through Thursdays. This works only if the rules apply to everyone in the house, including the parents.

• Try to make homework a pleasant experience—or at least not a totally aversive one. All too often homework time starts with a parent yelling at the children to do their assignments. The children are then banished to their rooms for a few hours and deprived of all human contact.

Instead, provide a lot of reinforcement for your children's studying, especially in the beginning. Drop by their rooms several times during a study session. Pat them on the backs or rub their shoulders. Bring them some popcorn or something to drink. After all, that's what we do when we're watching TV. Homework should be worth at least as much of a fuss.

Report Cards

The end of a school term is marked by celebrations, graduations, and, for almost all students from kindergarten through graduate school, report cards. Whether it is an old-fashioned handwritten folio or a computer-generated transcript, the response of both students and parents to this printed summary of teachers' evaluations is usually the same: a quick scan of the letter grades for As or Fs, followed by a sigh of relief, a yelp of excitement, or a muttered curse.

Despite their ubiquity, many educators question the usefulness of traditional report cards and grading schemes. Although they are supposed to provide feedback that will help children learn, measure children's academic achievements, and serve as predictors of children's later success outside school, report cards often meet none of those objectives. They are issued too infrequently to be a powerful reward for learning or a useful punishment for not studying. They are more likely to reflect a child's ability to parrot rote learning than skills at any more sophisticated form of intellectual activity. Finally, they are poor predictors of success outside the classroom.

Although psychologists and educators have repeatedly pointed out the problems and misinterpretations that commonly stem from traditional report cards, no alternative method of evaluating students' work has gained wide acceptance. There's enormous resistance to changing report cards despite their inadequacies. The typical categories and grading schemes are not significantly different from what they were at the turn of the twentieth century despite our vastly increased knowledge of effective learning, appropriate testing, and child development. Parents accept this lack of change with little hesitation, although they would be up in arms if automobile design or kitchen equipment showed similar stagnation.

One of the largest problems with traditional report cards is that they cause both parents and children to focus on the wrong things (such as their self-worth or general capabilities) when grades are low and to become inappropriately complacent when they are high. They encourage students, teachers, and parents to believe in "The Vaccination Theory of Education,"* which states, in essence, that a subject, like a vaccination against measles, is something you "take" and that once you've "taken" it, you can say you've "had" it, are now immune, and need never "take" it again. Report cards help isolate the skills of the classroom from the challenges and rewards of the real world, thereby reducing education to a series of academic hoops through which children must jump to get their promised rewards.

We can see the problems with traditional grading schemes and report cards by looking at what statisticians would call the validity and reliability of grades. The validity of a grade is a measure of whether it reflects what teachers think it reflects. Is the grade of B+ on a history paper a good measure of the student's knowledge of, or ability to interpret, a period of history, or is it really a measure of something else, such as the recall of selected dates or the ability to rephrase and incorporate the teacher's classroom statements? Once you've established what you're measuring, you must then look at the related question of how well you're measuring it, at its reliability. Would a variety of history teachers working independently give that same paper a grade of B+ (known as inter-rater reliability)? Would those same teachers, when asked to grade that paper two different times at, for example, six-month intervals, give it the same grade both times (test-retest reliability)?

The validity and reliability of traditional number and letter grades have been studied extensively since the early twentieth century with strikingly similar results. In essence, the studies show a great deal of inconsistency in the criteria teachers use to arrive at grades, thereby calling into question their validity. An

* Neil Postman and Charles Weingartner. *Teaching as a Subversive Activity* (New York: Delacorte Press, 1969).

A from one teacher may be a reflection of something totally different from an A from another teacher, even though the course is ostensibly the same.

Measures of reliability in grading have been equally disappointing. Although individual teachers are fairly consistent when asked to grade identical examinations or essays at six-month intervals, the consistency of grades assigned by different teachers to the same essay (inter-rater reliability) is much worse, with some teachers giving the same essay grades ranging from B+ to D−. (The results of these reliability and validity studies were so striking to researchers at the school of education at the University of Massachusetts at Amherst, where some of the work was done, that the school hasn't issued traditional grades since the late 1960's.)

All this points to the importance of not relying solely on report cards and examination grades for information on how well children are doing in school. An elementary school child who masters some arithmetic computations but not others may still do quite well at school—at least for a while. A shy child may receive higher grades because she is perceived as cooperative, just as a highly curious child who challenges a teacher's statements may receive lower grades because he is "obstructive."

The best source of information about how well things are going at school is your children. Talk to them not just about what they've learned or how well they did on a particular test but about how they feel about school. Which subjects are exciting and which boring? Ask them to teach you something they've learned, whether it is a song, a poem, or a beginning step in computer programming or differential calculus. This is a remarkably powerful technique that children often adore. After all, they spend so little time in positions of authority and power when they're with adults. It's also an excellent educational tool since it forces them to view the material they're learning from different perspectives. Often the best way to come to grips with a difficult subject is to try to teach it.

Read over your children's schoolwork occasionally. Look for ways you may be of help, especially ways that integrate the material your children are learning in different classes. One of the biggest problems with traditional education is that it fails to show the connections between English and mathematics and philosophy and art. If, for example, your children are reading H. G. Wells's *War of the Worlds* in English class or hearing in a social studies or psychology class about the 1938 radio broadcast of that story that terrified the United States, they should also look into how the book and the broadcast may be traced back to the poor translation of an Italian astronomer's scientific paper and to a civil engineering project in Egypt.* Remember that most children find adding a column of numbers or doing division problems boring but will get excited about balancing a checkbook or figuring out what's needed for two thirds of a cake recipe because those are adult tasks. Fractions are more easily digested when you get to eat the result of your labors.

How to Grade a Report Card

Despite the problems endemic to report cards, they may still serve as indicators of certain school problems and as reminders for both parents and children to assess how things are going at school. Here are some ways of making appropriate use of them:

• Use report cards as opportunities to review your children's progress with their teachers. Talk with all their teachers, not just the ones who gave them bad grades. This doesn't mean, however, that the report card should be the only trigger for a parent-teacher conference or telephone call. Remember that it's just as important to keep in touch

---

* This story is one of my favorite examples of why it's important to integrate material from different traditional academic fields to understand how the world works. It is a story that combines engineering, language, politics, psychology, and journalism in a way that even grade school children can appreciate.

In 1877, when Mars was at its closest point to the Earth, an Italian astronomer named Giovanni Schiaparelli tried to draw a map of that planet. He noticed what looked like dark streaks between larger patches of darkness. He called these streaks *canali*, an Italian word which usually translates as "grooves" or "channels." But the world was still fascinated by the latest human engineering achievement, the building of the Suez Canal, which had been completed in 1869. In the translation of Schiaparelli's work from Italian to English, the word *canali* became not "channel," which could occur naturally, but "canal." Since everyone at that time knew that it took great engineering genius to build large canals, the popular press and some scientists postulated that Mars must be inhabited by very intelligent beings. They also figured that since there were all these "canals" on Mars, the planet must have a water shortage. Wells latched on to this idea and made it the reason for the Martians' invasion of Earth.

with your child's school when things are going well as when they are going poorly.

• When you talk with your children about report cards, focus on their experiences in their different classes rather than on their grades. Instead of commenting only on the grades, ask them, "Did you learn anything that will be useful in your life? What did you think of who you were in that course? If you could do it over again, what would you do differently?"

• If you decide to reward your children for their performances, make the rewards contingent upon their behaviors, such as turning in homework on time, rather than upon their grades. Remember that lavish rewards are not necessary and may even be counterproductive if the child views the reward as the primary reason for behaving in a certain way. Simple praise, a treat, or extra privileges are often just as powerful.

• Variations in grades from course to course and semester to semester are to be expected from any child. Treat a significant drop in grades in several courses, however, as a warning sign that something may be wrong. Large drops in grades are often associated with depression, drug use, and dramatic family changes, such as divorce. In that respect, changing patterns of grades may tell a parent as much about a child's life outside school as about life inside school.

• Expecting perfection from your children always does more harm than good. Many children, especially those whose parents did well in school or who are doing well professionally, say that they feel as if their parents always want more of them. They see no point in doing better because they anticipate their parents' responding simply by raising their levels of expectation.

Self-defeating Behavior

Neither his parents nor his high school track coach understood what was going on. The boy did extremely well during practice, often performing at championship levels. The local papers were full of articles about his athletic potential and predictions of his success. Yet he did very poorly in competition. One day the boy brought a stack of newspaper clippings about himself to a psychotherapy session with a psychologist, spread them out, and said, "They're telling me to perform, and I won't!"

When the psychologist told me this story, I thought back to an eloquent description by John Holt* of elementary school students trying to predict whether weights on a balance beam would balance. The task involves an understanding of the concept of torque and the ability to multiply. A two-ounce weight placed six inches from the fulcrum or balance point will balance with a three-ounce weight placed four inches from the fulcrum. One girl in particular, when asked to set two weights so that they would balance, often placed them in positions that were clearly wrong. When asked to predict whether, once the holding pin was removed, the forces would be equal, she said they would not—even though the task assigned to her was to set them up so that they would balance.

She would rather accurately predict failure than risk trying for success and not achieving it, even when the negative consequences were the same in both cases. We see this all the time in both children and adults. A young aspiring actress and college student I knew had been given a much-wanted job in a Wisconsin summer stock theater but was so terrified of not being attractive enough for the ingenue roles (she was) that she gained about forty pounds before the season opened. That way she guaranteed her rejection since she could no longer be cast in the major roles, in which she might fail. I have known several writers who claim that they do not submit their work to agents or publishers because they might not be published. Yet by avoiding that risk of rejection, they have rejected themselves more harshly. We see the same patterns of behavior in many children.

Children who appear to be self-defeating are often fighting very personal battles for control over their lives. They are battles fraught with ambivalence and symbolic communications. Issues of personal control are most clearly seen in young chil-

* John Caldwell Holt, *How Children Fail* (New York: Pitman Publishing Corporation, 1964).

dren. A toddler, who has recently been punished for spilling something on the floor, will sometimes deliberately spill something again and then gruffly tell himself, "Now clean this up!" It is a way of telling his parents that he's going to take away their power over him by saying these things to himself.

Among adolescents the theme is the same, but the behaviors are more complex. A teenager who suddenly stops studying or handing in homework assignments has actually gained more power over his grades than when he was working hard. Yet if you ask that child why he isn't performing better, his answers will be vague or tangential: "I hate the teacher." "The class is stupid."

This is perhaps most common among children of upwardly mobile, ambitious, very intelligent parents. Success at school is so important to their parents that it becomes a focal point of the adolescents' rebellion. They believe that if they get B's in school, their parents will want A's. By getting D's and F's instead, they maintain more of a feeling of control over their lives as well as a needed separation from their parents. But the behavior pattern of self-defeating children is often quite different from others who are simply doing poorly in school. Children who sabotage themselves this way will occasionally hand in an A+ paper or exam and then, once the teachers' and parents' hopes are raised, go back to failing. It is another way the children show that they, not the adults who are pressuring them, are in control.

Self-defeating behavior can sometimes be rooted in fear rather than rebelliousness. A college freshman, who did well throughout high school, may be scared by the stiffer competition at his new school. He responds by not studying at all. That way he can convince himself that he's not really failing because he's not really working at it. It is more acceptable to fail that way than to fail after you've made a strong effort.

Abusing alcohol or other drugs is another way children sabotage themselves when they're scared they may fail. Showing up drunk or high for a test they're frightened of is a way to preserve their self-esteem. They can always blame that for their poor performance. Their real skills have never been tested.

Helping a Self-defeating Child

One of the most common responses parents have to a child who isn't performing up to his potential at school is to offer a reward if he improves his grades. It seems like a logical solution. Unfortunately it doesn't work. In fact, the more you promise, the more he'll work against your goals.

Remember that the issue is control, not grades. Many self-defeating children, especially adolescents, feel that they're valued by their parents largely for their successful performance. They say that their parents' self-esteem is wrapped up in how well their children do. By offering children rewards, you've further entrenched those perceptions and given them more control.

Instead, begin by asking yourself if you have ever communicated to your children that not being the best is tantamount to being the worst. Self-defeating children are often afraid of being rejected if they can't meet their parents' standards of performance. Explaining to your children that you value them for who they are rather than what they do—*and acting that way when they test you on it, as they surely will*—will help break the cycle.

Recognize that no child likes to fail. Children sabotage themselves when they see that as the least painful of their choices. Often that means that parents must change some of their behaviors. They especially must stop haranguing children about their grades. In one family, in which the parents of a teenage girl had spent thousands of dollars on tutors, remedial training, and psychotherapy to help correct her poor academic performance, the parents reluctantly agreed not to mention grades at all for six months. By taking away the battlefield, the girl could no longer use that as a way to show that she was different from her academically successful sister. The failures simply became painful. Consequently, she started doing better in school.

When you talk to your children about problem areas, such as school papers, don't focus on the quality of their work. Let the children set their own goals for their work. If they set their own goals, they can't get back at you by failing to achieve them. At the same time you can explore with them the consequences of failure, including being left behind when their friends move into the next grade. The prospect of being left behind by friends is a tremendously powerful motivator for children.

Perfectionism

The young woman, a twenty-year-old junior at a small southern college, told me that she attributes her straight A average at college to a great deal of dedication and hard work. Those efforts earned her several awards and scholarships, but she also feels sick a great deal of the time. She's had constant headaches for five months and has been seriously depressed.

She is a perfectionist and has been that way since the fourth grade. She lives in fear that her next paper or exam will receive an A −. She is majoring in a subject she doesn't enjoy because she knows she can get good grades in it. She dreads group projects because she knows the other students in her group will not live up to her standards. She cannot remember the last time she failed at anything. Her social life is nonexistent. "I'm almost twenty-one, and I've never been out on a date," she told me. "I guess I'm waiting for the perfect man."

Although there have been no studies of how common perfectionism is among children and adolescents, it is far from rare, especially among children with above-average intelligence. There are usually one or two in a typical class of twenty-five or thirty students, although few have the severe symptoms shown by the college student above. Many perfectionists have parents who are high achievers. The trait appears to run in families, although it is unclear how much is genetic and how much may be traced to the family environment.

Perfectionists live in a terrifying world of absolutes. A school paper is either perfect or worthless. A piano piece has to be played just so or not at all. Perfectionists *must* be the best at what they do or no one will like them. Paradoxically, their attempts at gaining control of their lives result in their abdicating all control. "I'm scared of failure," the college student told me. "If

I failed, I'd be letting myself and other people down. I've always lived my life for others."

While some perfectionists receive high grades, others do poorly in school. There are also children whose perfectionism appears in things other than grades. Children who have eating disorders, such as anorexia or bulimia, are usually perfectionists. Perfect thinness constantly eludes these children, almost all of whom are girls. They can never look quite good enough. They live on the border of starvation, furious at the bloated images they see reflected in their mirrors.

There is a certain safety in having unattainable goals. The paper that is never handed in is not, in the eyes of the perfectionist, a true measure of his or her ability. The painting that still needs a few brushstrokes cannot be judged. The report that is not begun until the night before it is due would have been better if the child had had more time to work on it. Perfectionists cannot finish their work because they want to make it perfect. Until they finish it, there's always the fantasy that they can write perfect papers or create perfect pieces of art. Once they've finished, they know they've failed, so they label their work incomplete and retain their illusion of control.

The first signs of perfectionism may start as early as age three or four. A mother told me that when her seven-year-old daughter was in preschool, she was afraid to write the alphabet for fear of doing it wrong. Now when she reads aloud, she hesitates, fearing that she'll make a mistake. Recently she wrote a letter to her grandparents and then cried for an hour because it didn't look as neat as she wanted.

For the past few years her teachers have been helping her be less demanding of herself. She no longer guards her dolls against the touch of playmates who do not treat them as she does. Her reading is becoming more fluid. "It's music to my ears whenever she says, 'I won't worry about it,'" her mother told me. "That's a good sign."

Helping a Perfectionist Child

Not all children who worry about details are perfectionists. For some children, spending hours building models or playing with dolls is a reflection of a growing sense of mastery. The key to knowing when there's a problem is whether the child is chronically worried. If children say the behaviors or the feelings are something they want to stop, it's usually a good idea to seek professional help. There are, however, some things that parents can do to help.

For many perfectionist children, a little reassurance, experience, and perspective help them rid themselves of their unrealistic expectations. Show your children that you're not perfect. Talking about the time you failed an exam or a course, didn't make a sales quota, didn't get the lead in a play, or were fired from a job may show children that everyone is allowed to fail.

While some perfectionists hand in twenty-page papers when the teacher sets a limit of ten pages, others apparently have the opposite problem. Perfectionism among school-age children often shows up as procrastination. Children may feel so overwhelmed by a school project that they delay beginning it until the evening before it is due. A little assistance with organizing can work wonders. Help the child break down the project into manageable chunks. For example, divide a paper into five sections. Give the child a small reward after each section has been completed.

Child perfectionists feel especially threatened when there is what they interpret as a significant change in the structure of their lives, such as going from elementary school to junior high or going away to camp for the first time. They no longer know what will be expected of them and fear that they will not live up to some unspecified and elusive standards. Spending time with such children reassuring them of their value to you and other members of the family may often be more effective than going over new schedules and procedures.

Finally, pay close attention to the consistency of the messages you give your children about perfectionism. It's often difficult to spot perfectionism or compulsiveness in ourselves, for we may describe such behavior in ourselves as "having high standards." When looking at the messages we give our children about perfection, we have to examine our own behavior as well as our words. If one parent is screaming at the other because dinner is at 6:33 P.M. rather than at 6:30, the child probably isn't going to pay attention to our reassurances.

Fear of School

Every morning during the first two weeks of seventh grade the boy tried to hide under his bed and fought off his parents' attempts to get him ready for school. He was so frightened of school that he thought about killing himself. It sometimes took his parents two hours to put clothes on their kicking, squirming teenager and drive him to school. By that time his first few classes were over. It wasn't that he was afraid of learning; it was that he just couldn't force himself to go into the building. The boy was suffering from a severe case of school phobia or school avoidance, a widely misunderstood problem that affects up to 3 percent of children in the United States.

Almost all parents have watched their children come down with occasional stomachaches or headaches that disappear as soon as the school bus pulls away. We may even remember having them ourselves. Such physical problems are one response both children and adults have to an overwhelming amount of stress. It is a way to substitute an acceptable and predictable pain for a situation that feels out of control. Even though there is no physical cause for the pain, the children's complaints and discomfort are real, as are their timely recoveries. In most cases their sense of control over their lives quickly returns. They are back in school the next day. This type of school avoidance is usually of little concern.

Among children who are school-phobic, however, the cycle of illness, anxiety, and fighting gets worse instead of better. The late-night stomach pains grow more intense. A few children even run low-grade fevers, yet when they are taken to the doctor the next morning, nothing appears to be wrong. Although many adults associate fear of school with children entering kindergarten or the first grade, studies have found that it's actually most common among eleven-year-olds. It occurs at the same rates and at the same ages in Japan and Britain as it does in the United States and is one of the few mental health problems to affect equal numbers of boys and girls. As with perfectionism, it appears to run in families, but it's unclear how much is genetic and how much environmental. In most cases, once it is recognized, it can be quickly and successfully treated.

School phobia is most easily recognized when it is brought about by a significant change at school, such as the transition to junior high or middle school. All of a sudden children have many teachers instead of one or two. Classes are much larger and contain different students in each course. Children are faced with many choices and much more responsibility. With those changes come stress and, in turn, a stomachache.

The problem may also be triggered by something apparently unrelated to the classroom, such as the illness or death of a parent or even a pet or a divorce. In these situations parents tend to be very sympathetic to their child's symptoms at first. After a few days they get angry because they feel their child is trying to get away with something. Neither the sympathy nor the anger helps. If the child is rewarded for missing school by being nurtured, the physical symptoms are reinforced and the stomachaches are likely to continue. If the child's behavior is met with anger, the anxieties increase, the stress level rises, and the physical symptoms get worse.

If Your Child Is Afraid to Go to School

Avoiding school is a symptom of a variety of childhood problems. It doesn't mean that your child has school phobia. The first step in helping a child who's reluctant to go to school is finding out what's causing the extra stress. This often takes a little parental detective work.

Is the child being ridiculed on the bus? Is his lunch money being extorted by larger kids? Is he terrified of being laughed at when he gives an oral presentation? One common fear among smaller children is of going to the bathroom at school because that's where the bigger kids pick on them out of sight of the teachers.

Among younger children a fear of school is often part of a larger fear of being separated from their parents. These children may be reluctant to sleep over at friends' houses or to go somewhere with other family members. Older children are more likely to be afraid of something specific at school, such as a bully or a new class.

Unlike school phobia, these more common concerns are rational and may be dealt with if the parents speak with school administrators or teachers. But children will very seldom admit to these problems directly. To discover the problem, try speaking to your child about how he spent the whole day away from home. Talk about it in vague terms, and look for nonverbal signals. Pay attention to when your child looks nervous or looks down at the ground.

When you think you know what's caused a problem, talk to your child about how he feels rather than about what's scaring him. Although most cases of school avoidance may be resolved without professional help, if the problem continues, consider bringing your child to a specialized clinic. Children are often more likely to talk to professional therapists than to parents about their fears since therapists are not as emotionally involved as the parents.

The bottom line of any treatment for school avoidance or school phobia is that the child must go back to school. The child simply must face the fear to overcome it. Keeping the child out of school for an extended period usually makes the transition back to the classroom more difficult. That also means that you shouldn't let your child get away with the things you did as a child. If your child's mystery illness clears up by 11:00 A.M., there's no reason why he shouldn't go to school for the rest of the day.

CHAPTER 9

Conflicts Between Children

THE TIMING and nature of the conflicts children have with each other may give us insight into what is going on in their minds. One of the most powerful ways in which children tell us their feelings and stages of social development is through their conflicts with other children. Children's awareness of teasing and their responses to it, for example, tell us not only about their self-concepts but also about their need to be part of a larger yet, from their perspective, exclusive group.

Parents who develop skills in interpreting children's conflicts with peers will be better able to help them overcome some of the most stressful times in their development. Friendship is a very important but novel concept for very young children. As they mature, the ways in which they establish and set boundaries for their relationships with peers help them get a grasp on who they are and where they fit into their world outside the family. Making friends is a skill that requires experimentation and practice. Many of the conflicts between children reflect that experimentation.

Understanding why ten-year-olds tease each other differently from five-year-olds and why children respond to bullies the ways they do will help you teach your children how to build relationships. Accurately interpreting what a child who's become a bully is telling you about social skills and self-esteem will help you teach that child more appropriate ways of handling social situations.

The clashes children have with each other are different from those they have with adults. Although a child who is throwing a tantrum may convince his mother, for example, to buy a toy he covets at that moment, it is clear to both parties where the real balance of power resides. Parents and children are not evenly matched. They both know that in the end the parents will win any conflict if they so desire.

But the rules and the odds are not the same for conflicts between children. The girl who calls her younger brother names and the boy who takes a toy from a playmate are behaving differently from the way they do when they are interacting with adults. Despite their apparent callousness, these battles serve a very important purpose for children. The bully and his victim, the teaser, and the aggressive child are each learning some of the rules by which the world operates. Learning to cope with verbal taunts, for example, is a very important skill for children to develop, as is suffering the consequences of inappropriate taunting. Dealing with a schoolyard bully is good practice for handling analogous situations as an adult.

The normal and understandable wish that your son or daughter live a conflict-free childhood is not only unrealistic but, more important, counterproductive. All children will, at some point, both tease and be teased, bully and be bullied, reject and be rejected. These experiences allow children to learn more about themselves. They allow the children to try on new roles and test new aspects of their own personalities.

Teasing

The ways children tease each other and the ways they respond to being teased can tell us much about their mental and emotional development. Beneath the taunting lie clues to how well children can think in abstractions and how well they understand the feelings and situations of others. Most important, teasing and being teased are ways for children to practice some of the social skills they will need as adults.

Teasing is universal. Anthropologists have found the same fundamental patterns of teasing among New Zealand aborigine children and inner-city kids on the playgrounds of Philadelphia. Like joking, teasing may serve two apparently contradictory functions when it defines the boundaries of a social group or clique. Most commonly, teasing is a way of threatening or rejecting outsiders. Yet teasing may also be a signal of social acceptance.

The most primitive form of teasing may be seen among toddlers as one child holds a toy in front of another only to pull it out of reach as the playmate's hand makes a grab for the prize. This physical teasing is more than simple selfishness. It is a test of relative power. The child has learned that what is mine is not yours—a surprisingly sophisticated concept.

Preschool children may find teasing very upsetting if it causes them to question some of the sense they've made of the world. If you tease a four-year-old child by saying that his red ball is actually blue, he will start to laugh. He has mastered the names of colors and therefore finds misnaming them tremendously funny—as long as both people know that's the game they're playing. But if you keep teasing a child that age by saying the red ball is blue, the child will become very upset and may start to cry. What began as a game is now terribly confusing to a child who is just beginning to struggle with the abstract concept that a color is something separate from an object. The thought that a red ball might be blue is simply beyond children's capabilities. An older child, who is better at abstract thought, would probably tease back by naming other colors or saying that it's not really a ball—or might simply decide that the game was stupid and the adult was not a good playmate.

Verbal teasing begins around age five. This stage of teasing often involves what the child considers "dirty words" (usually related to the bathroom) and is not triggered by anything in particular about the person being teased. Saying such things is, as children that age will tell you, simply being silly. While they may recognize that their teasing may arouse a parent's or another child's anger, they are unaware that someone might feel hurt by what they say. The other person's anger is obvious; sensitivity to creating hurt feelings requires more skill at empathy than they have developed.

This initial teasing helps children learn about the importance of context, discretion, and timing. Speaking to an adult at the dinner table with the same words they used on a fellow first grader at the playground may yield dramatically different results. Children quickly learn that they can get away with calling a classmate a dummy to his face, but the response is not nearly as benign when they say that to a teacher. Yet such teasing is often not malicious; it is a test of new and somewhat shaky social skills.

By the middle of grade school, when teasing has reached its peak, it has taken a different form. The verbal barbs are more pointed. Children who look or act different—the fat children or the ones with thick glasses—are frequent targets. The apparent viciousness of the attacks reflects not only the child's growing verbal skills but an innocence he has lost since he was a preschooler. He is more aware of his own weaknesses now, as well as the ways in which he is different from his classmates. Often, harsh teasing is a way he can build his own self-esteem by making someone else feel little and weak.

Young children will often tease another child either because they see something in that child that they don't like about themselves or because they're jealous of that child. This type of meanspirited and aggressive teasing starts to disappear in most children when they reach early adolescence. That change in the style of teasing is a sign that a child has become more empathic. Teasing someone because of physical appearance has now become awkward or even painful for the teaser as well as the victim.

At this point the nasty teasing is replaced by its adult form. It is no longer a challenge or a put-down but a way of demonstrating closeness. A friend can comment on an upcoming "hot date"; a stranger cannot. A family member can playfully criticize a choice of clothing; someone else using the same words would be considered rude and treated accordingly.

While a certain amount of teasing is perfectly normal, parents should become concerned if their children are using teasing as their primary or only way of relating to peers. That dependence on teasing indicates that the children need help with social skills as well as safe places to practice new ways of communicating with other children. Simply telling children not to tease is almost never effective, for they don't know what else they should do.

Many of these children are scared of trying new social behaviors with their peers. To them, changing their behaviors involves risking being laughed at or rejected, even though they may already be suffering rejections from their classmates because of the amount of teasing they're doing. New social skills are more safely tested in arenas where the children do not fear becoming embarrassed. That may mean role playing with parents or—and this can be particularly effective with some children—practicing with a pet dog, cat, or gerbil. Animals, as all children intuitively understand, never laugh at people when they make mistakes.

If Your Child Is Being Teased

Few things tug on the heartstrings of parents as much as hearing their child say how other people are teasing him or her. Yet many of the ways those parents respond may either make the situation worse or increase the time it takes to resolve itself. Here are some key points to remember in helping your child handle being teased:

• Telling your child to ignore the teasing is absolutely useless. Not responding will often cause the teaser to raise the ante by calling out a more painful taunt. Few young children can ignore this type of successive verbal abuse. When the victim finally reacts, he has lost the battle and is an easier target the next time.

• Don't belittle the incident. Tell your child that you understand that he's feeling hurt by the other child's words, even if those words aren't true. Remember that your child is also looking for reassurance that his relationship with you is still intact. Criticizing his response or telling him that his emotions are inappropriate will simply make him fearful that he has lost you as well.

• Pay close attention to what your child focuses on when he describes the teasing. If he focuses on the child doing the teasing, he may be scared of a bully or, if it's a friend, he may be scared of losing that friendship. If he focuses on the content of the teasing, he may need help bolstering his self-image. Talk with him about these fears and problems as well as about the teasing itself.

• Ask the child what he thinks the words that upset him mean, especially if the teasing was done by an adult or an older child. Sometimes children misunderstand words and assume that they mean bad things when they do not.

• Since the children most likely to be repeatedly teased are the ones who cave in to the treatment, the best solution is often to teach the child how to tease right back.

Remember that teasing is a skill that requires practice. The safest place to practice any skill is where you don't feel threatened and where you can afford to make mistakes. Do a little role playing with your child. Make the practice into a game. Tell him that the two of you are going to tease each other. See which one of you can come up with the most outrageous teases. Laugh about them, especially the ways in which he teases you. As little as ten minutes of practice can give a child the skill and confidence he needs to stop being victimized and to be better accepted by his peers.

Bullies

They are small acts of terror. The extortion payment may be milk money, the injuries limited to a black eye and bruised pride. Yet the young victims of bullies describe their ordeals in terms similar to those used by adult victims of organized terrorism. They blame themselves as they search for a logical reason for an illogical situation.

The child who is bullied will often hide his predicament out of shame. He will mention it to his parents only obliquely, testing the home waters for an emotional chill. It is better to pay the money and go without lunch than to risk being called a coward or a failure by someone close. Knowing when a child is being bullied, and responding to his needs, require an awareness of subtle changes in that child's attitude toward himself.

One mother told me how her ten-year-old son came home with a few bruises from a schoolyard fight. She knew that an older and larger child had attacked and threatened her son, but she assumed that the issue was settled since a teacher had told the bully not to bother the younger children. The next morning she overheard her son as he looked at himself in the bathroom mirror, whispering, "If I weren't such a nerd, nobody would hit me."

It was the child's way of testing how ashamed he should feel. The safest place to conduct that test was within earshot of his mother. Had she minimized his concerns, it would have reinforced his fear that he had caused the problem. He would have suffered in silence and isolation. Instead, she grabbed him and hugged him and told him over and over again that it was not his fault until he finally let himself believe her words.

Who becomes a bully? The roots of bullying appear to rest more in the child's home than his genes. Child development researchers at Indiana State University and elsewhere have found that parents of bullies tend to treat their children differently from the way parents of other children treat theirs. Parents of bullies don't appear to use nearly the amount of humor, praise, or encouragement that other parents use when they talk to their children. Instead, they use more put-downs, sarcasm, and criticism. Very little of this appears to be malicious or even conscious on the part of these parents; they are often very frustrated and upset by their children's behavior and would very much like to help their children learn to behave more appropriately.

Parents of bullies also tend to touch their children differently. While the average parents touch their children to show affection, the parents of bullies use touch to control their children. They are more physically manipulative and forceful. Because touch gives a mixed message to these children, they have more trouble interpreting what is happening when a parent touches them. Bullies also tend to see the world as more threatening than it really is and are likely to misinterpret the actions of other children. If a child unintentionally bumps into a bully, the bully will probably interpret the bumping as aggressive instead of accidental.

Bullying is a growing concern to mental health workers and educators, for studies indicate that bullies do not outgrow their problem. If they are not helped, they are more likely than other children to have trouble in school, drop out of school, and be involved in criminal behavior.

The most successful way to change bullies involves working with their parents at least as much as with the children themselves. While the parents learn ways to handle conflict without yelling and hitting, the children are helped to develop their ability to empathize and shown how to be assertive. This latter treatment is often surprising to many adults. The last thing these children need, they reason, is to learn how to stand up for themselves. Although assertiveness training is usually thought of as a help for timid or shy children and adults, it has shown to be especially helpful for bullies since these children go from being passive to being aggressive or hostile without intermediate steps. The assertiveness training gives them an alternative to aggression as a way of getting what they want.

Teaching Your Child to Handle a Bully

Although parents can usually recognize the difference between a bully (who poses little real threat) and a serious attacker, such as a mugger, children often cannot. To a second grader, a student in the fifth grade who is demanding a quarter can appear formidable. Although it is important to help children learn to stand up to bullies, it is equally important that they learn when they should not fight, such as when another person has a weapon.

Television programs and movies make heroes of people who stand up to armed robbers. Hundreds or even thousands of times children have seen people use a few quick moves to disarm and turn the tables on attackers. This gives many children the idea that they could do so as well. Reality, of course, is different. Let your children know that if they are mugged by someone who is armed or who is much bigger than they are, you will be disappointed in them if they try to fight back. Help them gain a sense of perspective about fighting over a few·dollars.

With bullies, however, the situation is more psychologically stressful than physically dangerous. All children should know that they can go to an adult in authority, such as a teacher, if one is nearby. If there's no one around, the best reaction is probably a series of escalating responses— beginning by ignoring the bully. Unfortunately many bullies are very good at taunting children in ways that make them react.

The next step is firmly telling the bully to stop and letting him know that you won't tolerate what he's doing. Bullying is based on the belief in form over substance. The bully believes that by acting tough, he will be regarded as powerful. Simply by assuming an air of authority, a smaller child may be able to get the bully to leave him alone. If the bully continues, if there is no adult around, and if the child cannot walk away from the situation, more direct action is needed. If the bully isn't much larger than the victim and the bully hits him, the child should hit back. It's a response that the bully doesn't expect, so it may stop the attack.

Much to the surprise of young children, most bullies may be stopped before they do the things that they are threatening. This is especially true when things are not going according to the bully's plans. (That is why hitting a bully once after he hits you will often stop the fight immediately.)

I remember having several encounters with bullies when I was growing up. Every time I had the courage to stand up to one, the bully backed down. (There were times, I'll admit, when my courage was not as resolute as was my concern over being beaten up.) Once when I was in high school in New York City, a bully in my class was snapping a towel at other boys in the locker room. When he hit me, I grabbed the towel from his hands and told him to stop.

This clearly embarrassed him. To save face and to maintain his self-image, he told me he wanted to fight. I said no. He then said he'd meet me outside my apartment at five o'clock that afternoon. I said no. A crowd was gathering around us. He asked me if I was too chicken to fight him.

I said no, but that I wasn't going to do so. The realization that I, not he, had taken control of our interaction and that his bullying tactics weren't working clearly frustrated him. He turned bright red, stomped out of the locker room, and never bothered me again.

Aggressive Children

There are times when even the most docile children appear to have the aggressive tendencies of a professional wrestler. While a certain amount of pushing and shoving is to be expected from all children, especially when they are very young, there are a few for whom aggression becomes a way of coping with almost any situation. These overly aggressive children are not bullies; they often get into fights with people who are stronger than they are. They face problems not because they are aggressive but because they become aggressive at times that are inappropriate and in ways that are self-defeating. They routinely argue with teachers and wind up in far more than their share of schoolyard scraps.

According to Dr. Stanley Turecki, a child psychiatrist in New York City who specializes in helping the families of what many development experts call difficult children, in some cases this pattern of overaggressiveness appears to be rooted in the children's developing nervous systems. They appear to be physiologically unable to control their impulses as much as other children their age. For others, it is often a matter of needing to learn and practice social skills.

Aggression is one of the first responses to frustration that a baby learns. Grabbing, biting, hitting, and pushing are especially common before children develop the verbal skills that allow them to talk in a sophisticated way about what they want and how they feel.

Children are often rewarded for their aggressive behavior. The child who acts out in class generally gets the most attention from the teacher. The child who breaks into the line to go down the slide at the playground sometimes gets to use the slide the most. One of the toughest problems parents and teachers face in stopping aggressive behavior is that in the short term it gets the child exactly what he wants. It's only after a few years that inappropriately aggressive children must cope with a lack of friends, bad reputations, and the other consequences of their behavior.

For some children, this tendency toward physical aggression and other difficult behaviors appears to be inborn. There's some evidence that a proportion of these children may be identified as restless fetuses that kick significantly more than other fetuses. Many very aggressive children are noted to be restless infants even before they begin to crawl and walk. These overly aggressive children appear to have less mature nervous systems than other children their age. This shows up in a variety of problems with self-control. They cannot sit still for more than a few minutes. They are easily distracted. Once they begin to get excited or angry, they have difficulty stopping themselves. They are impulsive and have trouble concentrating on a task for more than a few minutes or even seconds.

Coping with a Very Aggressive Child

It's difficult for adults not to attribute malicious motives to children who consistently appear to be trying to drive their parents and teachers to distraction. Often it's equally difficult for parents not to assume that children are behaving this way because of something the parents have done wrong or have forgotten to do right. Such casting of blame, however, is not only inaccurate but usually useless as well.

The first step in helping an overly aggressive child is to look for patterns in what triggers the assaults, especially if the child is a toddler or preschooler. The aggression may happen only at home or only in public places. It may occur mostly in the afternoon or when the child is frustrated. Also, most of these children go through a predictable sequence of behaviors before they lose control. It's a bit like watching a car going through a normal acceleration and then suddenly kicking into overdrive.

Once you've determined the most common triggers and can spot the escalating behavior, the simplest thing is to remove the child from that environment before he loses control. Take him away from the sandbox or the play group for a minute or two until he regains his composure. As the child develops, he will become less frustrated and, therefore, less aggressive because he has a wider variety of ways to respond to a challenging situation.

It's also very useful to provide these aggressive and distractible children with a lot of structure and routine in their daily lives since predictability helps children remain calm and in control. Tempting as it may be at the time, spanking these children for being aggressive often does more harm than good. It is simply modeling the very thing you don't want children to do. It teaches them that big people hit when they're angry or upset, and that is precisely the aggressive child's problem.

For older children and adolescents, teaching new and more appropriate ways of getting what they want can be very helpful. These children often have not learned the more sophisticated negotiating techniques and other social skills that their classmates picked up years earlier. As with bullies, formal assertiveness training can be particularly helpful to overly aggressive children since they have difficulty distinguishing between assertiveness and aggression.

It's also useful to help these children look at life from a slightly different perspective. Psychologists have found that both aggressive children and their parents tend to focus on what's wrong with a situation rather than what's right with it. That makes their respective problems all the more frustrating for each of them, since neither pays any attention to the children's improvement when it occurs.

Rejection by Peers

Being rejected is an integral part of growing up. No child escapes the occasional brisk slap of exclusion from a group. For those children whose long-standing reputations proclaim that they do not fit in, the painful sting of rejection comes often. It may permeate their views of themselves and lead to problems during adolescence and adulthood.

An occasional rejection of a child by classmates is usually nothing to be concerned about. One study of third graders showed that about half the children who were rejected by their peers were able to correct the problem by the following year. However, when the child talks for several months about being taunted or ignored, it is usually time for outside help, for such chronic rejection can lead to more serious difficulties.

Studies at Vanderbilt University in Nashville have found that by the time children are eight years old, about 8 percent of boys and 3 percent of girls are socially rejected by their peers. Such chronic rejection is usually associated with behavior problems and is a good predictor of a variety of later antisocial problems, such as juvenile delinquency, dropping out of school, and criminality in adulthood.

Although aggressiveness is the most common reason children develop bad reputations and are rejected, it is by no means the only one. Even among those children who are described by their classmates as aggressive, studies show that only about one in three is highly disliked. Why are some children accepted by their peers while others gain bad reputations and are shunned? The common denominator is the lack of positive social skills, such as how to initiate and maintain relationships and how to resolve conflicts with other children.

The most common approach to helping children change their reputations is to train them in new and effective social skills. Individual coaching and supervised practice in such fundamental techniques as sharing, waiting their turn in line, playing according to rules, and responding appropriately to teasing are often effective in helping rejected children gain acceptance. Sometimes, however, even such new behaviors are not enough to change long-established reputations.

If children see someone they think is a bully who is acting kindly, they don't think, "Gee, that kid isn't a bully anymore." Instead, they look for things that match their preconception. Experiments at Waterloo University in Ontario in which children had to make judgments of their peers support this conclusion. Students in the second, fifth, and tenth grades were told a story in which a classmate did something bad to them, such as making fun of them when they dropped their books. Half the time the classmate was someone the students liked; the rest of the time it was someone the students said they didn't like.

Students in all three grades were more likely to give the child they liked the benefit of the doubt. If it was someone they liked, they explained the behavior by saying things like "He wasn't trying to make me feel bad. He was trying to cheer me up." If it was someone they disliked, they were much more likely to say, "He was doing it to be mean. He's always mean," even though the behavior was exactly the same.

When Your Child Is Rejected

Your nine-year-old comes home in tears. After going through a dozen tissues and a half dozen cookies, he recounts how the other kids called him a jerk and won't play with him. How should you handle the situation?

First and most important, don't overreact. Even though your child is in no condition to believe this, you should remember that most of these situations are short-lived. Simply acknowledging that it hurts to be treated that way and restating your love and support will often take away most of the emotional sting the child feels. (The cookies help, too.)

Although it's awfully tempting, don't try to be a public relations agent for your child by taking the other children aside and telling them that they're being unfair, even if the rejection has gone on for several weeks. Such an approach is often useless at best and counterproductive at worst. It gives the children yet another reason to reject your child. Remember that this isn't a court of law. You don't have to disprove the other children's allegations.

Instead, look at the occurrence as a sign that your child needs some help with the skills needed to make friends. Surprisingly, it's sometimes as simple a matter as your child not seeing you having fun with your friends, so he doesn't have any models at home to guide him. Some schools and many child guidance centers offer programs that help children learn and practice such friendship-building skills as sharing feelings and cooperating. School activities, such as theater projects or group presentations in which children rely on each other rather than compete, can be very helpful. You can reinforce these new cooperative behaviors by praising your children effusively when you see them trying out the skills. Don't worry for the moment about whether they are doing them well. It's more important that they simply try these new approaches to relating to other children.

Even so, well-established reputations are difficult to change, especially when a child tries out these new behaviors on more than one child at a time. Often the changes are ignored, the child becomes frustrated and lapses into old patterns, and the rejection continues. Remember that it's usually easier for a child to break through rejection and establish one-on-one relationships than it is to enter a larger social group. Having classmates come over individually to play is more likely to change the perceptions of the group and less likely to be frustrating.

CHAPTER 10

Sibling Rivalry

THE BONDS between siblings are unlike those between other members of a nuclear family. There are no rituals, such as marriage or anniversaries, that mark their start and continuity. Nor is there a legal equivalent of divorce or disownment by which siblings can formally sever their ties.

Dealing with siblings poses unique challenges and opportunities for children. They are playmates and coconspirators, competitors, and teachers. To many parents, the most frustrating aspect of their children's relationships is their rivalry. Preschoolers and school-age children take careful note of who got to ride in the front seat of the car the last time the family went out or whose chocolate chip cookie has the most chips. Their words, anger, or level of competition appear out of proportion to the issues. The intensity of the rivalry often, at first, makes little sense.

The key to interpreting what is going on requires that we look past the cookies and car seats and squabbles over who really gets the most attention from Mom or Dad. Instead, we must view sibling rivalry as a powerful communication from our children about how they view themselves and their world. Understanding why children treat their brothers and sisters the way they do, and what you can do if that rivalry appears to be getting out of hand, are among the most challenging aspects of being a parent.

The Essence of Rivalry

Rivalry during childhood often sets the tone for the relationship siblings have as adults, but not in the ways many parents think. When things go well, the squabbles over toys and battles for attention that punctuate the lives of young children and drive their parents to distraction may in fact be the tools by which brothers and sisters learn to be close as adults.

There is a certain safety in testing authority or practicing verbal put-downs on a brother or sister, for both siblings know the relationship will transcend the remark. Not all conflicts between siblings are good, of course. A child who is repeatedly humiliated or made to feel insignificant by a brother or sister is learning little except humiliation and shame. Verbal sparring matches, however, help children recognize when their "clever" comments cut too deeply. They learn when to be assertive and how to compromise. This pattern of combative behavior is seen on a simpler level among young animals, especially apes, as they try to hone their newfound social skills by wrestling with and screaming at each other.

Studies conducted at the University of Hartford have shown that the closer the siblings are in age, the more intense the positive and negative parts of their relationship are likely to be. Siblings spaced less than five years apart, according to this research, had either closer or more turbulent relationships, both as children and as adults. Siblings with greater age gaps had less opportunity for conflict as near equals. Their relationships tended to be emotionally more distant.

Although sibling rivalry is inevitable, the incessant bickering, yelling, and hitting that mark some relationships between brothers and sisters is not. To put sibling rivalry in perspective, it's useful to look at a few techniques actors and playwrights use in conveying their characters. Part of the task of an actor is to show how his or her character relates to the other characters in the play. Much of this is done through a form of visual and verbal shorthand, using behaviors that quickly establish how each character feels about the others. An actress who gives one character a peck on the cheek and another a passionate kiss has quickly established their respective relationships in ways that we all can understand.

One of the most difficult relationships for a playwright to craft and an actor to play is that of a friend. How do you show that relationship? Are you "nice" to the other person? Are you continually supportive? Such approaches almost always make for poor characterization and a boring performance. A much more effective and compelling approach is to find ways to compete with the other person. How do you fight with the other character over the check after dinner at a restaurant? When the other person tells a funny story, do you try to tell one as well, vying for the attention of the others onstage? At the core of every friendship is a certain amount of rivalry.

We know what that friendly competition looks and sounds like among adults. That is why this approach to character development works in the theater. A friend can get away with making a sharp comment or insult that a stranger or mere acquaintance cannot. A friend can tease you about things that are off limits to others. There's a certain paradox to this. The people who insult, criticize, and tease us the most—the behaviors that, at first blush, we might assume would come from our enemies—are our friends. We cannot assume, therefore, that children who treat each other to barrages of insults, criticism, teasing, and the occasional left jab really dislike each other as much as it appears.

The Symbolism of Rivalry

Before you can be effective at taking the edge off sibling battles, you have to be able to analyze what's going on by looking for and interpreting the signs your children are giving you. A few are obvious, such as the seven-year-old who starts wetting his bed when a new baby arrives. Others are much more subtle and can display a symbolic elegance that rivals poetry. It is the symbolism that is important and, quite frankly, the most fun to analyze and dissect.

Almost all the behaviors that parents describe as sibling rivalry are highly symbolic. Take the common situation in which a six-year-old gets upset that you're using "her" baby blanket on her newborn sister. Arguing the logic of the situation ("You're too old and too big for this blanket anymore. It doesn't even fit your bed. You have your own blanket") misses the point by focusing on the content of the child's words rather than on the feelings. From a six-year-old's perspective, giving her younger sister the baby blanket she used as an infant means that she's being replaced. It is a thought that so terrifies a child her age that she cannot verbalize it directly and must use symbols. The easiest response is equally symbolic: Give your older child back her baby blanket, even if she cannot use it. Acknowledge its importance, and tell her that it will be hers for the rest of her life.

Stepping back and looking at the symbolism may help in many other instances of sibling rivalry. Your eight-year-old son, Bobby, runs into the kitchen and tells you that Max, his ten-year-old brother, just hit him. The older boy quickly follows and says that Bobby ruined a computer game he was playing.

PARENT (*very frustrated*): "Why can't you two get along? I can't leave you alone for thirty seconds without your going for each other's throats!"

BOBBY: "He's a bully! He hit me even though you told him not to."

MAX: "Well, he won't leave me alone. Make him leave me alone."

PARENT (*resigned to the inevitable*): "OK, which one of you started it this time?"

BOBBY AND MAX (*in unison*): "He did!"

Variations on this interaction probably occur tens of thousands of times per day. Each child feels righteously indignant while the parents try to assign blame and vent their own frustration. The problem with this approach is that it cannot resolve the situation in a way that is satisfactory to more than one of the parties involved. If the parent simply separates the children, they will be miserable. If either Max or Bobby is declared the one who was right, the other child will look for ways to get even and will continue being disruptive.

Parents in this situation often feel frustrated not only with their children but with themselves as well. You want to be peace-makers and feel as if your efforts are to no avail. Compounding the problem, you may feel angry at the older child, who is teasing and taunting, or upset with the younger child for not having the wherewithal to handle the problem alone. Such feel-ings are natural and to be expected. Sibling rivalry may be a very stressful situation for the entire family, not just the chil-dren involved. The first step in handling those feelings is to analyze what's really going on and what role each of the par-ticipants is playing.

Despite the best of intentions, parents are often so emotion-ally close to the rivalry that they may inadvertently contribute to its continuation. Asking bickering children which one of them started the fight is not only a fruitless endeavor but one that focuses on the wrong issue. It attempts to turn one child into a winner and the other into a loser. All that does is give the loser another reason to start the next fight so that he or she will be declared the winner of that round. It simply perpetuates the cycle. Similarly, blaming the children in vague terms or asking rhetorical questions like "Why can't you two get along?" aggra-vates the problem rather than solves it. It fails to acknowledge the legitimacy of their feelings at the time. Children who are told that they can't get along will tend to believe it and act accordingly.

Instead, step back from the situation, analyze the symbolism in the children's actions, and look for ways they can behave that will be less disruptive. Keep in mind that you cannot force siblings to be close. At best, you can help them develop the skills they need to become close to other people, such as empathy, patience, and tolerance of differences. Children perceive adults, especially their parents and teachers, as very powerful beings. It is extremely rare that a child will go to another child and complain that his older brother just hit him. Clearly, then, there is a special purpose served by going to a parent with the prob-lem.

The child who says, "He hit me!" is far less concerned with

the punch than he is with establishing his dominance in more important matters. Parents have been his protectors and have demonstrated their love by shielding him from harm. There is great symbolic power in being protected by a strong and loyal army of supporters, even if they never strike a blow. Running to his parents is, at its core, a political gambit aimed at grabbing power, at least temporarily. The other child recognizes the gambit, of course, since it is one he has used himself. He tries to counter his brother's arguments with more of the same. "He ruined my game. [Therefore, oh powerful one, you should support me since my cause is just. Together we will squash the infidel and live happily ever after!]"

The same sorts of ploys are seen when children argue over what appear to be trivial things. "Her cookie has more chocolate chips than mine does!" "Why do you always kiss her good-night first?" (In some families the complaint is that you always kiss the other child good-night last, showing that anything you do can be a trigger for competition between siblings.) Trying to be "fair" or to do things "equally" is a hopeless endeavor, as parents who try it soon discover, because it focuses on the words instead of the symbols. Children will search for the inequality, no matter how small, because it allows them to gather more information about how you feel about them and how secure they are in their family.

The complaint about the cookie or the order of good-night kisses is often no more than a cry for reassurance that the child is loved. It is a question that should be answered directly and repeatedly. But telling children that you love them isn't enough. Children often express their inner feelings indirectly. (Adults do this as well, of course.) They are often unaware of how acceptable those emotions are. Since children often confuse the acceptability of their feelings with the acceptability of themselves, these strong emotions can be distressing.

The child who complains that you're spending all your time with the new baby or that her older sister called her "stupid" is often testing whether her parents still love her despite her strong emotions. Parents who respond by telling the child to ignore the name-calling or who deny the child's emotions by arguing over how much attention they give the older child are missing the child's hidden question. Instead, parents can acknowledge the existence and appropriateness of each child's emotions.

The boy who's jealous of the new baby will usually perk up if his mother says something like "I know that you don't like my paying so much attention to your baby brother." The girl who's been teased will respond to "I can see that it hurts when your sister calls you names." In each case the child's feelings have been recognized, and the unasked question—"Will you still love me if I feel these things?"—is answered.

One of the most common ways parents try to avoid or defuse sibling rivalry is by treating each of their children in exactly the same way. Unfortunately not only is this impossible, but it will tend to aggravate problems with sibling rivalry since it gives children a yardstick by which they can measure their relative worth in your eyes. If you give a child a bicycle when she's five, don't feel obligated to give her younger brother a bike at the same age. Similarly, don't give children of different ages the same privileges, such as staying up until a particular time. The older child will be resentful of the younger one's shared status. The younger child will value the privilege less because it came so early.

Instead of trying to do the same things for all your children, focus on their individual interests and talents—an act that lets each of them know that you're really paying attention to who they are and that makes power struggles more difficult. Arranging for piano lessons for one child and gymnastics lessons for the other (that is, if each is interested in the tasks) may make both of them happier than if they had to compete in yet another arena.

The question still remains, of course, of what you should do to keep siblings' complaints about unequal cookies, punched shoulders, and ruined computer games from getting out of hand. Remember that even the most sophisticated use of the techniques in this and other books will not stem all rivalry between siblings. That's not such a bad thing since a certain amount of sibling rivalry is very useful for learning how to build strong relationships. That having been said, here are three basic guidelines for handling sibling rivalry:

• Look beyond the children's words to see what is at the heart of the problem.
• Work with your children on developing acceptable behaviors.
• Involve your children in developing ways of reaching those acceptable behaviors.

We've already examined the importance of looking for symbolism in a child's complaint. The second guideline requires a similar ability to look past the words the children are uttering. Most parents, when asked their goals in handling sibling rivalry, think in terms of negatives: "I want them to stop fighting." "The older one shouldn't tease his younger brother." While those words accurately and vividly describe the parents' goals, they say little about the behaviors they want from their children. They are focusing on negotiating a cease-fire in the prolonged battle going on at home.

Instead, think about the skills you would like your children to learn. Should they be able to resolve minor conflicts without resorting to violence or coming to you for help? Should they learn to take turns selecting what they should do together? Would you like them to be more tolerant of each other's needs? Once you've decided on your first goal, look for behaviors you could use to measure it. The things the children do that you find annoying, such as yelling at each other, usually will provide excellent clues. Once you have decided on a behavior you'd like to change, your next step is determining a way of measuring the changes in that behavior.

Let's say that the most important challenge you'd like to address is helping your children learn to resolve minor conflicts without resorting to violence. The obvious behavior you want to decrease is hitting. One measure of your success will probably be the number of times per week one of your children comes to you with the complaint "He hit me!" The catch is that your children have to share this goal, although they may not share it for the same reasons you have. If they don't see any value in decreasing the amount of hitting, they won't have any reason to cooperate.

If stopping the hitting isn't enough of a reward for them, at least in the beginning, you're going to have to come up with something that is. It doesn't have to be big, but it must be something that can be objectively measured. Saying, "I'll spend more time with you," is too vague. For example, you might make an agreement with your children that if they can go a week without complaining about being hit, you will take them both out for ice-cream sundaes. If you hear only one complaint during the week, you'll take them out for ice-cream cones. Two complaints means no ice cream. Three or more complaints means no television or some similar restriction for a certain number of days. It's important, of course, that both children like ice cream (the easy part) and do not want to lose their television-watching privileges (a safe bet) and that the rewards and punishments are always given to both of them so that they cannot become part of the power struggle. It doesn't matter who did the hitting or who started the fight. Also, they probably won't simply continue the hitting but stop the complaining because their complaints are now more powerful.

Once your children have been successful at not hitting and not complaining to you, you can begin tapering off the rewards by increasing the necessary battle-free time periods. Eventually less hitting will become rewarding in and of itself, and your children will probably stop asking how many more days before they get their sundaes. You can expect your children to test you when you start this type of program by hitting each other, complaining to you, and seeing whether you'll fall back into your old habits. This type of testing is actually a good sign. It shows that they're paying attention to the program.

The third step is to involve your children in developing ways of achieving your shared goals. Young children, especially, are used to having little power within their household. Solving problems is, in their eyes, a highly coveted adult job. Consequently, almost all children will rush at the chance of developing a solution to an important problem. By participating in that process, they become highly motivated to show that their solution can be successful.

In your attempts to decrease hitting at home, ask your children for their suggestions. Judge those suggestions at least as much by your children's enthusiasm for them as by your estimate of their probable effectiveness. Many solutions that appear ludicrous to adults may actually work very well with children. One of your children may suggest, for example, that you agree on a secret code word like "marshmallow" that means all hitting has to stop. If it's your children's idea and they're enthusiastic, it will probably work.

Quick Tips for Handling Sibling Rivalry

Parents often have more control than they think when it comes to forestalling the development of destructive and lifelong rivalries among their children. A few tricks of the trade, such as paying extra attention to the older children when a new baby arrives or giving them doll "babies" to play with, are obvious. Others are more subtle and can often be remarkably effective.

• Ask an older child to tell you what she thinks the new baby is feeling. Is the baby hungry or happy or cold? Ask the child how she would feel if she were the baby. That helps even toddlers identify with a new rival and understand that a baby has emotions much like their own.
• With older children, pay more attention to them when they're cooperating and less attention when they're fighting. Although this is more easily said than done, the times when parents should be rewarding children with attention are often the very times when they leave children alone.
• Remember that if you fight with your children to get them to stop fighting, they'll remember what you did, not what you said. Help younger children understand the changes their older brothers and sisters are going through. An eleven-year-old boy may be confused by the reasons his thirteen-year-old sister wants more privacy and doesn't pal around with him the way she used to. Explain her growing need for privacy and her interest in boys her own age.
• Recognize that the apparent absence of sibling rivalry can be a sign of trouble. This is most frequently seen when one child has a physical or mental disability that requires more of the parents' attention. The other child may take on the adultlike role of care giver to the disabled sibling, yet harbor a great deal of anger and guilt about the rela-

tionship. Encouraging some healthy competition in an area where they can compete equally can help release those hidden frustrations.

Stepsibling Rivalry

At first the two eight-year-olds treated each other with the wariness of two hungry cats that suddenly have to share the same food bowl. They had, until David's father decided to marry Kay's mother, each spent most of their lives as the only child of single parents. Now that was changing. David and his father had moved into Kay's home.

The teasing, tattling, and tussles that routinely mark sibling rivalry can become a special problem for blended families. "Only" children have to learn to share a parent's affection and attention. Cries of "Mom always liked you best!" can have a sharp and bitter edge to them. Parents often feel as if they were being tugged in opposing directions by their feelings of love and protectiveness for their spouse and their children.

Children undergo a large number of dramatic and subtle changes when they enter a blended family. Parents often underestimate the extent and importance of those changes.

Private space is a major area of conflict for stepsiblings. The dickering over who gets which bedroom or who has to share a bedroom can make political negotiations in the Middle East pale by comparison. If, as is often the case, one side of the family moves into a house or apartment that the other side has been living in, the territorial squabbles can grow very bitter. The children who are already in the house and who already have their own turfs staked out feel imposed upon and threatened. The entering children feel more out of place than their new stepsiblings.

Birth order becomes confused in blended families. Most children define their roles within the family partially in terms of where they are among their siblings. After a remarriage a girl who has been the oldest child for ten years may suddenly have two big stepsisters. A boy who was the baby of the family suddenly loses the advantages of that position to a stepsibling.

Holidays can become arenas of strong conflict for blended

families, especially for the first year or two. Each set of children, unsure of what the new family means for their future, clutches at the past by insisting that its is the "right" way to celebrate. Christmas trees are divided in half so that each set of children can decorate it "properly."

Age plays a major role in determining how children respond to their new families. Teenagers often have more difficulty than younger children in adapting to blended families. Parents wonder if the apparently rebellious adolescent who stays away from the house and doesn't participate in planned family activities is trying to sabotage the new family.

Often the problem is not the child's attitude but a conflict between the stage of development of the child and the stage of the new stepfamily. Separating from family and developing an individual identity are among the major developmental tasks of adolescence. It is important that teenagers place some distance between themselves and what they perceive as the dependent behavior of their childhood. Spending time with friends away from home and arguing over parental restrictions are ways of safely testing the turbid waters of adulthood.

The newly formed stepfamily, however, is at a developmental stage much closer to that of a younger child. Parents strive for the new family to be surrounded by the symbols of harmony and closeness. The adolescent perceives those same symbols as signs of the very dependence he is trying to escape. The more the parents promote togetherness, the more the teenagers strive for separation, both from their parents and from their new stepsiblings. By recognizing a teenager's desire to spend time away from family and with friends as a sign of normal development, rather than by forcing the child to spend time with family, parents can help their children form bonds with the new family in the most appropriate and long-lasting ways.

High school seniors and other teenagers who are about to leave home may have a very different reaction to a parent's remarriage from that of younger adolescents. While a fifteen-year-old may rebel against the new family, an eighteen-year-old will often embrace it. The soon-to-depart child is often relieved that someone else will be able to take care of his or her parent.

Before trying to put a stop to all stepsibling rivalry, recognize that, as with other forms of rivalry, some aspects of it are very healthy. The competition allows children to practice some new roles. It also allows them to figure out for themselves the types of relationships they want with their new family members. If you try to turn them into an all-loving instant family, the children will simply rebel by showing you how much they can't stand each other. Remember that your strongest ally is time. Give your children and yourselves a chance to stumble about a bit as you sort through the new relationships.

Helping Stepchildren Adjust to Each Other

When I wrote a newspaper column about how newly blended families adjust to one another, I interviewed several psychiatrists, psychologists, directors of organizations for stepfamilies, and stepparents themselves to get their advice. I expected them to focus on complex psychological issues involved in creating a new family. Instead, each began by emphasizing the importance of practical matters, such as who moves into whose house or apartment. Both the therapists and the parents said that the decision of where to live and how to set up living arrangements may be critical to the success of a new family.

Here are some of their suggestions:

• If it's financially feasible, move the blended family to a home where neither side has lived. That avoids much of the feeling that one side of the family has invaded the territory of the other children, who must now give up something they believe is theirs.

• If you can't move to a new house or apartment, at the very least make sure that each child has some private space—ideally, but not necessarily, a bedroom—that's inviolable. Battles over who gets which bedroom can be settled by having children rotate bedrooms each year. In one family I know, the two eight-year-olds fought to get the bedroom that was close to where their parents slept. Neither wanted the bedroom that was isolated. Now that they're teenagers, they both want the one that's far away from their parents. Switching rooms every summer has settled the problem.

• Encourage and respect the children's differences. Referring to them as "the boys" or "the girls" often breeds resentment instead of togetherness.

• Join a support group for stepfamilies. There are several national organizations, such as the Stepfamily Foundation, Inc. (333 West End Avenue, New York, New York 10023), and the Stepfamily Association of America (215 Centennial Mall South, Suite 212, Lincoln, Nebraska 68508). Community organizations such as the YWCA often run support groups as well.

Finding the right group may take a bit of shopping around. Not all groups are of equal value, and even the best ones may not meet your family's needs. In addition to trading information on dealing with problems, it's often worth joining just to keep reminding yourselves that you're not alone.

• Finally, share your history through photographs, home movies or videotapes, and family stories. Let the new members of your family know how you got to be who you are.

The New Child in a Blended Family

A woman I once interviewed for a newspaper column told me that it can take her several minutes to describe the biological and legal links between the children in her life. She brought two children from her previous marriage to her current one. Her husband brought three from his earlier marriage. They have had two children together. Her ex-husband also remarried and had a child by his second wife.

Parents in stepfamilies who are considering having another child often wonder what the effect of the new baby will be on their children from previous marriages, their stepchildren, and their current marriage. Studies of these complex relationships can offer some guidelines for predicting the special benefits and problems that often accompany children who are born into stepfamilies.

Parents in a blended family who have a child will often report that the other children started feeling much closer to one another and to their stepparents now that they all had a relative in common. That sense of closeness is less likely to occur, however, if the new child arrives soon after the new marriage, according to both researchers and family therapists. The normal feelings of jealousy and anxiety children have over the birth of a sibling are compounded by their adjustment to the stepfamily. They sometimes feel that the new child is more entitled than they are to a position in this new family. Similarly, parents may feel easily overwhelmed by the number of changes in their lives if the child comes soon after the new marriage.

One study of fifty-five remarried families by Dr. Anne Bernstein, a psychologist at the Wright Institute in Berkeley, California, found that not all children respond equally well to the addition of a baby to their stepfamily. The children who had the most difficulty coping were between the ages of six and nine, had been their parents' only or youngest child, and were in families in which the baby was born during the first four years of the remarriage. The younger the children were at the time of the remarriage, the more readily they accepted the stepparent and the new baby. Those children who adapted most successfully were preschoolers and early adolescents.

The birth of a baby to an ex-spouse or a noncustodial parent raises very different issues. Adults sometimes respond by feeling a sense of mourning for their former marriages, as if the arrival of children by their former partners' new spouses end any hidden hopes of reconciliation. A new child tends to increase the emotional distance between a divorced couple. Children, for their part, sometimes feel angry or frightened. Despite the marriages of their biological parents to new people, many children harbor the unrealistic fantasy that someday they all will get together again. New babies shatter that fantasy. The children may also fear that since their noncustodial parents— usually the fathers—have new wives and new babies, they won't need their old children anymore.

Helping Children Adjust to the New Baby

There are several things parents and stepparents can do to help children adjust to a new child in their blended family:

• Be sensitive to issues surrounding the child's last name. Children may sometimes be distressed that the new child's last name is the same as only some of theirs, but not all of theirs. Because of this, those children who have a different last name may not feel as close to the baby as their stepsiblings do.

• Recognize that children will watch all their parents and stepparents carefully for cues about how they should respond to the new baby. Correcting a child by saying, "He's not really your brother; he's your half brother," or making similar comments that reinforce the distance between them will emphasize the difference in the baby's status within the family. Young children may feel very threatened by that.

• As a parent you can usually expect to feel differently about a child you've conceived with your spouse from the way you do about your stepchildren. The "mutual" child is often a sign of commitment to the new relationship or a symbol of a second and possibly last chance at becoming a parent. Many parents in this situation report that they feel especially close to this new child. There's nothing unusual or inherently bad about that.

• Involve all the children in the preparation for and care of the new baby. Be especially conscious of including the children who don't live with you since they are more likely to feel threatened by the idea that the new baby is replacing them in your eyes.

• Pay close attention to what the introduction of a new baby does to your family's life at home. It's easy to become so wrapped up in the new child that you don't pay as much attention to the small rituals and celebrations of the other children and of your spouse.

Only Children

The decision to become a parent begs the obvious next question: How many children? For many, especially those parents unsure about whether to have one or two children, it is a question not easily answered. A growing number of parents in this country are consciously choosing to have only one child. The number of women who are having their first children in their thirties and the increasing rate of divorce after only a few years of marriage are also leading to more families with only children. Are these parents making a mistake?

Common knowledge holds that only children are at a serious disadvantage when compared with children who have brothers and sisters. They are allegedly more lonely, selfish, spoiled, and maladjusted. Their parents are sometimes given similar labels. The preeminent American psychologist at the turn of the century Dr. G. Stanley Hall stated emphatically, "Being an only child is a disease in itself." The parents of only children are constantly asked when they will have another child and told how much better that would be for both children's development. After all, how else will their child learn to share? How will he or she learn to relate to other children? Indeed, a study conducted during the height of the baby boom in 1956 found that the most common reason parents gave for having a second child was to prevent their first from being an only child.

"But wait," cry the supporters of only children. Franklin Roosevelt was an only child. So were Hans Christian Andersen, Indira Gandhi, Elvis Presley, and Jean-Paul Sartre. (It may, in fact, be the *only* list in which those five names appear together.) Doesn't this mean that only children have an advantage? Aren't only children more likely to achieve greatness than their friends who have brothers and sisters?

In fact, say psychologists at the American Institutes for Research in Palo Alto, California, and at the University of Texas at Austin who have been comparing only children with children who have siblings, it's all a myth. The differences between "onlies" and other children is too trivial even to consider, especially when compared with differences like sex and economic status. While some studies show statistically significant differences between groups of only children and groups of children with siblings, many of those differences may be accounted for by problems with the designs of those studies.

A disproportionate number of only children, for example, live with single or divorced mothers. Because of this, differences in family income or social status may have influenced some results more than the number of siblings. Even when such factors are controlled and the differences between the two groups of children are still statistically significant, they may not reveal any practical difference, as when one group has, on average, a fraction of a year more education or slightly higher self-esteem than the other.

Still, a child with brothers and sisters has experiences that an only child may not get at home. The child from a larger family must learn to share more of the attention his parents pay and may gain some maturity and sense of responsibility by helping care for younger brothers and sisters. That's why it's especially important to get an only child involved with a regular play group of other children before he starts school. For many only children, group day care allows them to build their skills at dealing with other children from an early age.

CHAPTER 11

Fighting with Your Children

Ghosts from the Past

A friend who works as a commercial artist told me about a recent incident. She had had a rough day at work and was, by her own admission, in a foul mood when she got home from work one afternoon. As she walked through the kitchen door, the first things she saw were several piles of dirty dishes near the sink and a milk carton sitting on the counter.

She became furious. Hadn't she just told her children to put away their things when they were through with them? Why did she work so hard and then have to come home to such a mess? She grabbed the nearest child and started screaming.

"All of a sudden I heard my mother's words come out of my mouth," she confessed with a look of amazement on her face. "They were the words that I swore, as a child, I would never say to my own kids. But I was really angry. I know that when I get angry, the things that I say are the things my mother said to me."

All parents carry similar baggage from their own upbringings. No matter how much we disliked yelling, spanking, nagging, or manipulating as children, and no matter how ineffective these approaches were, they sometimes seem the only thing to do.

By understanding what triggers these gut-level responses, you can often avoid being on the other end of the battles you fought as a child. Or you may decide that what your parents did wasn't so bad after all, for some of the battles between parents and children provide a means for those children to grow socially and emotionally. A few even appear to be programmed in our genes. To children, fighting with parents is another means of communicating when they don't know the words to express what's happening in their lives. The challenge for parents is to decipher the message. It is especially difficult because arguments are by definition emotionally stressful. (I must confess that I envy people who are skilled at seeing and responding to these hidden messages. I've found that it's a lot easier for me to do this with other people's families than with my own. My personality is such that when dealing with my own family, I tend to become caught up in the emotions and rhetoric of arguments and to forget, in the heat of battle, all the things I'd advised others to do.)

Many psychologists report that parents often first catch themselves doing or saying something they didn't expect when their child is between sixteen and twenty-four months old. That timing is no coincidence. At first glance, much of a toddler's behavior is confusing. She will throw her food on the floor as soon as her parents tell her not to make a mess. She will reach for a forbidden object, such as an electrical outlet, and then tell herself "No!" before pulling her arm back.

Behavior like this, which soon disappears, is a sign that the child is developing an awareness of herself as an individual. She is also trying to figure out the difference between what she *can* do and what she *should* do. (That's why you'll sometimes see a toddler do something wrong and then scold herself for doing it. She's figuring out how those two concepts fit together.)

If you understand that those developmental issues are the reasons for a toddler's apparent defiance, you're less likely to take her negative behaviors personally. It is not a rejection of your love or a challenge to your authority. It is simply a way the child prepares herself for independence. Parents who don't understand what's going on are more likely to respond emotionally by resorting to yelling or spanking.

Such gut-level responses are most likely to be triggered by certain types of battles with children. In many ways, however, the apparent topic of the argument is irrelevant. The real issue for both sides is likely to be who is in control.

Control is a major issue for all children, but especially for toddlers and adolescents. It doesn't matter whether a parent is telling a two-year-old to take a nap or a thirteen-year-old to be home from a party by ten o'clock. If you told the two-year-old to eat his spinach or the thirteen-year-old not to go to the movies, the fighting would be the same.

Battles for control often degenerate into what psychologists call a zero-sum game: For a parent to win, the child must lose, and vice versa. All attempts to reach a compromise are dropped as each side tries to undermine the other. Brute force—the kind we remember our parents using—usually wins. "You'll do it because I say so!" Both parent and child are left feeling angry and frustrated.

Falling into this trap every so often is normal and nothing to worry about. Problems occur when the parent-child relationship turns into a never-ending cycle of power games and rebellion in which parents repeatedly fall back on primitive means of asserting their control. That is when parents become habitual users of the same techniques they hated when they were children. Screaming, spanking, hitting, or inducing guilt becomes the most common way they communicate with their children.

Parents who come to rely on these primitive responses are seldom nasty or malicious. More likely, they are very frustrated. They don't know how to interpret their children's behaviors, and they can't think of anything else that would work. Children who grow up in these environments learn that bluster and physical force are the primary ways of getting what you want as an adult. Yet these are the very tools they used as toddlers. They are also tools that do not work very well when the person you're fighting is larger than you or can simply walk away. Children who learn more sophisticated methods, such as negotiation, have a broader repertoire of useful approaches to problems and are more likely to be successful at getting what they want.

Breaking the Cycle of Arguments

It can be extremely difficult, in the heat of a battle with a child, to stop yourself from saying the same things that you've said to that child before and that, perhaps, your own parents said to you. Our emotions can run so high that we're in the middle of a fight before we're fully aware of all the things that led up to it. Although catching yourself before that happens is ideal, for many people—myself included—it's almost impossible.

One way to break out of what seems like a never-ending cycle of fruitless arguments with your children is to keep a diary or log for several weeks. (To me, this is as boring and frustrating as writing out a financial budget, but it really does work.) Every time you feel things have gotten out of hand, write down what happened, what you were feeling before the incident, when and where the problem occurred, how you interpreted your child's behavior and how confident you are of that interpretation. If your child is old enough, explain why you're keeping the diary.

In most cases you'll begin to see a pattern after a week or so. Things may get out of control only when two children are vying for your attention, when you're out in public, or when you come home from work.

Look for ways to interpret your children's behavior that don't assume they are being malicious toward you. A two-year-old may be physically unable to eat as neatly as you would like. A teenager may choose certain clothes because they're worn by classmates he or she admires. Assuming that it's done to spite you will bring about only frustration and inappropriate reactions.

If your daughter is making a mess in the kitchen, it may simply be a way to get your attention. Listening to your yells may be the price she's willing to pay to get the attention from you that she needs. (If that's the case, she is really paying you a backhanded compliment. How many of your friends would listen to you scream at them simply because they wanted to be with you?)

Test your hypothesis by paying more attention to her

for things that don't involve making a mess. At the same time, praise her for cleaning up the dishes she used. Often that's enough to make her realize that she'll get more attention—and less painful attention—by cleaning up than by leaving a mess. (You may have to be a bit sneaky when you do this and not tell her what's going on since if your hypothesis is wrong, and possibly even if it's right, sharing your interpretation of her actions may cause her to sabotage your plans.)

Also, turn your children into allies by making the problem the enemy. Let them know that keeping the diary has helped you figure out which situations cause you to do things you later regret. Ask them to come up with some solutions. Some of the best solutions are remarkably simple, such as leaving notes to themselves to clean up the kitchen before you come home.

There's another advantage to involving your children. If they have developed a possible way out of the problem, they're more likely to give it a try than if you simply tell them it's another thing they have to do.

The Benefits of Fighting

Arguing with children is as much a part of being a parent as nurturing them. There's a beneficial side to the fights you have with your children. It's a side that's seldom discussed, but it has drawn the attention of a growing number of researchers. Fights with toddlers, if they are handled well by the parents, may actually help the children prepare for school. The battles with teenagers over cutting their hair or cleaning up their rooms appear to be much more complex than we thought. The timing of these battles tells us a great deal about not just our own children but perhaps the history of our species as well.

The number of arguments between parents and children usually increases at two critical times in the children's development: the so-called terrible twos and the early teens. Recalcitrant two-year-olds are learning some very important skills when they battle you over finishing their food or putting on their socks. The reasons for the more frequent arguments with a teenager may have more to do with biology and evolution than anything you've done as a parent. Last night's fight over taking out the garbage may, in fact, be a response to a problem people faced thousands of years ago.

Two-year-olds, much to the frustration of their parents, often respond to any request by saying no. As with the things they find funny, their acts of defiance tell us a great deal about the issues they are struggling with. By that age the idea that they are individuals separate from their parents is firmly entrenched in their minds. Now they are flirting with the concept of power. Phrases like "Me do it!" and "Mine!" become a regular part of their dealings with you. They no longer obey without question.

The rebelliousness of a two-year-old is different from the obstinacy of an adult or even an older child, for toddlers cannot understand the consequences of their actions. It is also such a necessary part of their development that children who do not rebel may be telling you that something is very wrong.

The rebellion of a two-year-old can take any of several forms. Each approach appears to reflect, in part, how parents treat the situation. Research on toddlers done at the University of Guelph in Ontario has shown that parents who use direct commands or force are more likely to have children who are openly defiant. Parents who use suggestions and explanations have children who learn to use a primitive form of negotiation.

If you have insisted on immediate obedience from your child in the past and now ask her to finish eating her string beans when she doesn't want to, she'll probably tell you, "No!" and may even throw a tantrum. If, on the other hand, you sometimes explain why you want her to do things and if you every so often let her win a battle, she's more likely to reply to the string bean gambit by saying something like "I already ate one."

But a toddler's negotiations are, however, much less sophisticated than they appear. In many ways, the content of the dispute is irrelevant, as are many of the logical arguments frequently offered by frustrated parents. Two-year-olds can't understand abstract concepts like good nutrition. They are simply testing how the world will respond to their newfound power.

By practicing negotiating with their parents over such things as string beans and nap times, toddlers appear to be learning skills that will serve them well in kindergarten and elementary school. Several studies indicate that those toddlers who have practiced only open defiance to authority may have more trouble with the give-and-take needed in making friends and working in groups. Those who have learned to compromise may have an easier time handling the structure of school since they will have the skills needed to cope with the increased structure and competition.

How to Sell Your Five-year-old a Used Car

Rare are the parents who have not felt their blood slowly boil as they listened to their preschooler yet again refuse to cooperate with the simplest tasks. She won't eat the carrots because they're cut wrong. He wants to wear his cowboy shirt even though it's in the wash. The more you insist, the more obstinate they get. You say no. They whine. You yell. They cry. Everyone's upset and miserable.

The next time you're negotiating with a preschooler, remember the wisdom of the car salesperson. As any good car salesperson will tell you, there are times when a little chicanery or sleight of mouth is needed to convince customers to do something that they are resisting. Hundreds of books have been written about ways to "close the deal" or get the customers to do what the salesperson wants them to do and to think that it was their idea all along.

One of the most popular approaches is known as the major-minor close. The salesperson wants the customer to say, "I'd like to buy that Chevrolet at the price you're asking for it." The customer, however, is reluctant to make that commitment, even if he or she really wants the car. If the salesperson asks directly, "Would you like to buy that car you've been test-driving?" the customer may very well say no.

Instead, car salespeople will ask their customers if they would prefer the cars in red or in blue. Would they like the radio with or without a cassette recorder? Would they prefer to finance their cars through the dealership or through their bank? By the time the customers have finished answering these "minor" questions they have committed themselves to the "major" question. By agreeing to get the cassette recorders, they have bought themselves new cars.

In addition to making you a more savvy car shopper, remembering this approach can often help you cope with a child who seems bent on making your life miserable by quibbling about small decisions.

A friend of mine used to have arguments with her five-year-old daughter every morning. The script went something like this:

"Why aren't you wearing your red pants?"

"I want to wear my green dress."

"But it's cold outside. That's a summer dress."

"I don't like my red pants. I want to wear my green dress."

"OK. But you'll have to wear tights to stay warm. Hurry up! The school bus will be here any minute!"

"No tights! I want to wear socks and my party shoes."

"You can't wear the party shoes to school. They're for parties. Besides, I said you could wear the dress. Why do you always do this?"

And so it went. The child became angry. The mother became frazzled. They each dreaded the morning confrontation. Eventually the mother realized that she and her daughter had two different goals during the daily ritual. The mother wanted her daughter to dress in appropriate clothing. The girl wanted to have some freedom of choice in what she wore. Being five years old, she didn't understand why certain clothes were more suitable for specific seasons or occasions. She only knew what she liked.

To achieve her goal, the mother did what any good car salesperson would do: a major-minor close.

"Time to get dressed. Would you like to wear your red pants or your blue pants?"

"I like the blue pants."

"Do you think they'll go better with the plaid sweater or the yellow sweater?"

"The yellow sweater is prettier."

"Do you want yellow socks to match the sweater or blue socks to match the pants?"

"Yellow."

Before the child knew it, she was dressed in the type of clothing her mother thought was appropriate. Both mother and child had accomplished what they had set out to do.

As powerful a technique as this is, however, it doesn't always work. I recently read about a kindergartener who, for a period of time, insisted on wearing several layers of skirts to school. Her mother sent a note to the child's teacher saying that the child's taste in clothing "does not necessarily reflect the clothing tastes of the management."

The second peak in parent-child arguing occurs about a decade later. The trigger for this new wave of rebelliousness appears to have less to do with a child's age than with the churning of hormones. Psychologists have noticed an increase in fighting when a child reaches puberty. The chronological age of the child doesn't seem to matter. If puberty comes early, so does the arguing. If it comes during the mid-teens, that's when the number of arguments goes up. Few of these battles are over large issues such as drugs, sex, and plans for the future. They are more likely to be about the child's cleaning his room or taking out the garbage—mundane issues in everyday life that triggered the arguments we had with our own parents. To an adolescent, it is these types of issues that symbolize independence.

Biologists have noted a similar pattern of fighting (although, one presumes, about different topics) between adolescent apes and their parents. This may, at first, appear to be a bit of esoteric information that's good only for cocktail party chat or game shows on television. The fact that a similar pattern appears among animals, however, provides both researchers and parents with some very powerful information and a good bit of insight into what's probably going on with teenage children.

Among the best models for this behavior are gibbons—small apes that swing from tree to tree with energy and enthusiasm that would put an aerobics instructor to shame. When baby gibbons reach puberty, they leave home to search for gibbons that are outside the group. If they do not leave voluntarily, their parents will have very vocal fights with them and eventually throw them out of their home.

Zookeepers describe a related behavior among marmosets and other monkeys raised in captivity. Young females do not develop sexually if their mothers are kept in the same cage. Once the adolescent marmoset's mother is removed from the cage, the child becomes sexually mature within a matter of days.

All the fighting between sexually mature gibbons and their parents and the suppression of hormones in adolescent marmosets kept close to their mothers appear to be ways of preventing inbreeding and the genetic problems it causes. But what does this have to do with your children? Surely human beings behave differently.

The next time you hear a twelve-year-old say that he wants to leave home, realize that that's exactly what children at his stage of hormonal development did until a few hundred years ago. Before the Industrial Revolution most adolescents left home about the time they reached puberty. (Because of better nutrition and general health, children in the United States reach puberty about four years earlier than they did a century ago.) These "placed-out" children often lived with adults who were not their parents. The practice is still common in some nonindustrialized societies.

The bickering and squabbling between parents and adolescents may actually be more a reflection of our evolutionary history than a battle over taking the dog for a walk. That's an extremely important concept because it suggests that such fighting may be inevitable. No matter how good a parent you are, increased arguments during a child's puberty appear to be bound to happen. Not only that, but the intensity and style of those battles may be determined, in part, by how well your child learned negotiating skills during his first fights with you over string beans when he was two years old.

Fighting Successfully with Your Adolescent

The fact that there appears to be a genetic component to certain fights with adolescents doesn't mean that parents shouldn't or can't do anything about them. At its best, a fight is little more than a problem-solving session with the volume turned up. It's also a way for teenagers to test and assert their independence. With those things in mind, there are some specific approaches that work very well in bringing arguments with older children (and adults) to a successful resolution that solves the problem:

• Establish the ground rules for a fair fight. This is, of course, better done before the fight begins. Talk to your children about what rules they think might be appropriate, such as no name-calling, no sarcasm, allowing each person to express an opinion, and not making statements that begin with emotionally laden phrases like "When I was your age . . ." or "But everyone else gets to. . . ." The rules, of course, must apply to everyone, not just the children.

• Agree to define the problem. It's frustrating for everyone (especially me, since it's happened to me many times) to realize, after a half hour of yelling and screaming, that you haven't been talking about the same thing. Agree ahead of time that you'll allow each person to state the problem as he or she views it. To a child, an argument over how late he can stay out on a weekday night may be a challenge to his maturity. To one parent it may be a matter of safety. To another parent it may be a matter of responsibility or being alert enough for schoolwork. Simply arguing about the time doesn't address any of these issues.

• Agree to be creative. Do a bit of brainstorming. Don't reject ideas from any party to the argument even if those ideas appear to be outlandish. Building a new wing onto your house or renting a second apartment for your teenager is not likely to be an appropriate solution to the problem of his messy room, but it may lead to something more practical, such as buying some extra furniture for storage or creating space by donating some of the extra clothes in his closet to the Salvation Army.

• Agree to table some issues. The brainstorming session may point out some areas where you each need to do some research. For example, who manufactures an inexpensive storage device that both you and your child think would help keep his room neater? (There are inexpensive nets that hold light items such as stuffed animals in a corner of a room by the ceiling. A used two-drawer filing cabinet may help keep a student's desk better organized.)

• Don't limit yourself to one solution. Almost every solution to a problem is more difficult for one person than the other. If anyone feels that a solution is unfair, it leads to resentment and sabotage. Solutions are more likely to be successful if they involve more than one approach. Finding additional storage space in another room, throwing out or giving away unwanted clothes and sports equipment, buying a small storage cabinet, and limiting parents' comments about the messiness can serve together to solve the problem.

• Make sure your approaches are measurable. This is easy with such things as buying a storage cabinet. It's more difficult when it comes to giving away clothes or limiting parents' comments. Agree to determine ahead of time how you will know if an approach has been successful.

• Set a timeline. Agree to a time when you can evaluate your solutions to see if they've worked. Throw out the approaches that have failed, and if necessary, try some new things.

How a Little Mathematics Can Help You Avoid Years of Guilt

Please don't turn the page! I realize that the last thing you expected to find in a book about child development was a section on mathematics. When I give lectures, a lot of people cringe when they hear me mention mathematics and parenting in the same breath. (I was tempted to title this section something like "The Secret Way to Make Five Million Dollars Tax-free in Ten Days" just so that you wouldn't skip it.)

Just bear with me for a short while. By the end, at the very least, you'll have learned some terms that will impress your friends and neighbors when you casually use them at parties. If things go well, you'll avoid years of unnecessary anxiety and guilt over some of the decisions you make about your children.

There really is a link between child rearing and mathematics. To understand the connection, you have to overlook the obvious differences and focus on the similarities between raising a family and such diverse tasks as manufacturing automobiles or running a stockbrokerage or managing a restaurant. The key to that connection is in the approaches you take to making decisions.

Parents have to make a lot of decisions. Are the children ready to go to kindergarten? Should they each get a haircut a week before they appear in the annual Christmas pageant? Are they responsible enough to take a city bus downtown by themselves? Do they have to finish their vegetables at dinner?

Automobile manufacturers also have to make a lot of decisions, which at first glance appear different from the ones parents make. Should they decrease the number of welds on the chassis? Which manufacturer should they buy springs from? How many people should be working the night shift this Thursday? No factory manager would consider making such decisions without doing a bit of statistics or, as they like to describe it, "crunching a few numbers." As parents, of course, you won't have any numbers to crunch. What's important here, as far as making decisions about children, are not the numbers but the logic and thought behind them.

To see how statisticians approach a problem, let's begin with some assumptions and a decision. Assume that you're poor, you love chocolate, and you work as an apprentice plumber. A local alchemist who moonlights in a candy shop has told you that if you heat five pounds of a very special chocolate until all that is left is a charred powder that you then sprinkle over a lead pipe, the lead will turn into gold. The alchemist also sells you five pounds of his very special and expensive chocolate. Your decision is whether to eat the chocolate (which is absolutely delicious) or to char it with your butane torch and sprinkle it on the pipe. You'd give the alchemist's formula a fifty-fifty chance of working.

Statisticians would begin analyzing your situation by saying that your "hypothesis" is that sprinkling the pipe with the ashes will turn the lead into gold. They would also look at the two types of errors you might make when deciding what you should do. Statisticians, who are usually more creative with numbers than with words, refer to these by the clever names of Type I and Type II errors.

You make a Type I error when you accept a false hypothesis. If you decided that you should char and sprinkle the chocolate and all you were left with is a dirty lead pipe, you've made a Type I error.

A Type II error occurs when you reject a true hypothesis. If you decided to eat the chocolate and, unbeknownst to you, the ashes *would* have turned the lead into gold, you've made a Type II error.

You could outline the problem like this:

Hypothesis: The charred chocolate can turn lead into gold (50 percent confident).

If I do it and I'm wrong (Type I error): Empty stomach, wasted chocolate, dirty pipe.

If I don't do it and I'm wrong (Type II error): Full stomach, missed opportunity, clean pipe.

Decision: ??

This approach to problem solving bears a closer look because it can help you put parental decisions in perspective. For example, is your son old enough to go downtown by himself using public transportation? You're only 50 percent certain that he can handle it alone.

Parent's hypothesis: My son will be safe (50 percent confident).

If I let him go alone and I'm wrong: My son could be seriously hurt or become very frightened.

If I don't let him go alone and I'm wrong: My son will be angry at me and may act in a way that I find annoying.

Decision: Don't let him go alone.

"Aw, Mom!" he whines. "All the other kids go by themselves! You never let me do anything. . . ." But the answer is straightforward. Since the perceived risk is so great, your son has to convince you that he is able to handle the task of traveling alone. If he can raise your confidence in your hypothesis, you will be more willing to risk making a Type I error. Whining doesn't raise your confidence. Neither does the fact that some of his classmates allegedly travel alone.

Together you can decide what your son can do to show that he can handle the task. That might involve making smaller trips alone or other specific ways he can show his sense of responsibility. Since changing your decision will be based upon what your son does rather than who he is, whining or pleading can't induce guilt and regrets.

Let's take another example. You want your daughter to wear her new dress to a family gathering. She wants to wear something else. The more you insist on the dress, the more she digs in her heels.

Parent's hypothesis: My daughter should wear a dress to the gathering (99 percent confident).

If I insist that she wear a dress and I am wrong: My daughter will be properly dressed and also angry at me. I'll never hear the end of it.

If I let her wear what she wants and I am wrong: My daughter will be improperly dressed, and I will feel uncomfortable about it.

Decision: Let her wear what she wants.

Even though the odds of your hypothesis being right are so high, the disadvantages of insisting on the dress outweigh the disadvantages of letting her wear what she wants. In other words, it isn't worth the hassle. You have more important things to worry about. Life's too short.

CHAPTER 12

Illness and Death

I WAS five years old, and I knew that I had caused my father's cancer. We had played softball in the backyard several times that summer. He would slowly pitch the ball toward me, and I, with predictably poor results, would swing a wooden bat at it as it flew past. One time, however, I managed to hit the ball squarely. My father was apparently not prepared for my success, since the ball hit him in the solar plexus and knocked the wind out of him. I was scared as I watched this big and powerful man grasp his stomach and try to catch his breath.

A few months later my parents told me that my father had to go to the hospital for an operation on his belly because he had developed cancer. Immediately I remembered my father doubled over and gasping for air. I knew it was all my fault; I should never have hit him with the ball. Since neither of my parents mentioned the incident, they obviously didn't know I was to blame. I felt frightened and ashamed and unable to tell them. It was my secret that I dared not share.

My guilt festered for a few weeks until my mother, who was a pretty good amateur psychologist, noticed that while my father was in the hospital, I had become uncharacteristically quiet and passive. She asked me if I thought I had been the cause of the problems. I nodded and haltingly told her the story about hitting my father with the softball. She listened without interrupting and then, without belittling my fears, explained that my father's cancer was definitely not caused by being hit by a softball.

Illness and death are among the most difficult topics to discuss with children. We try to protect them from the pain and suffering of others in the hope that they will enjoy their short-lived naiveté. Despite these good wishes and intentions, illness and death play a significant role in many children's lives.

How Children Interpret Illness

Children respond to sickness within a family very differently from the way adults do. The innocence that protects children from sharing the distress of older people causes its own problems. These problems are fairly predictable, however, for they reflect the stages of a child's emotional and cognitive development. The elaborate fantasies of a preschooler, the strange questions of an eight-year-old, and the embarrassment of a teenager tell us about the issues they each are struggling with at that time in their lives.

Preschoolers live in a world filled with magic and populated by powerful and omniscient adults. The fairy tales and other stories they adore reflect their fascination with enchantment. A kiss can turn a frog into a prince or awaken a sleeping princess. A special incantation can open the door to a cave filled with treasure. To a four-year-old, these images are no less credible and no more magical than seeing water spring forth from a drinking fountain at the press of a button or hearing music playing from a radio. As adults we understand the difference between the wave of a magic wand that turns a pumpkin into a coach and images that appear when we turn on a television or an automobile that starts when we turn the ignition key. We understand enough about the physics of the television and the automobile—at least at an intuitive level—to explain what is happening without believing in supernatural powers.

This difficulty preschoolers have distinguishing fantasy from reality may be seen in what psychologists call magical thinking—the idea that giving voice to a thought can make it happen. Such thoughts have a simple logic all their own that adults sometimes fail to appreciate. They also reflect the child's fundamental belief that he is, in effect, the center of the universe and that objects and people—especially parents—exist primarily to serve and protect him. Many three-year-olds will tell you, for example, that the sky gets dark at night because that's when they want to sleep. Until the child becomes older, discussing the earth's rotation on its axis is fruitless and, from the child's perspective, irrelevant. They want to go to sleep, so the sky becomes dark. It is magic.

This unquestioned belief in magical powers distorts a young child's perception of illness within a family. A five-year-old who remembers saying to a parent, as all children do, "I hate you! I wish you were dead!" may believe that those words caused the parent's illness. To preschoolers, the logic of the situation is irrefutable. They said the magical incantation and are now facing the results of their unintended power. It is a story they have heard again and again in such tales as "The Sorcerer's Apprentice."

Although this belief in magical powers tempers as children grow older, children under the age of about eight frequently view their parents as omnipotent. This, too, causes problems, for the thought that an illness is stronger than their parents can be especially terrifying because of its implications. If parents cannot protect themselves from illness, they cannot protect their children from harm. When a parent is ill, these children become scared of things that have little apparent connection with the illness. They may regress in their behavior, suddenly wanting to sleep with night-lights, sucking their thumbs, or wetting the bed. Through these actions they test their tentative hypotheses and their fears: "Am I still loved? Am I still safe?"

That's why lying to children about an adult's—especially a parent's—illness can backfire. It is more than just a matter of the children's sensing the tension in the household. Instead, the mixed messages they receive reinforce their apprehensions. These children have their worst fears confirmed: "The world is once again unpredictable. We can no longer trust the adults in our lives."

Even older children who view their parents more realistically can harbor unrealistic fears. Those fears may be expressed directly or, as is often the case with young children, obliquely and in ways parents sometimes find disturbing. Their behavior, in fact, may appear precociously adult and look at first as if it were a sign that the children are handling things well. It is, however, a mask for their true feelings and fears.

These stoic children may feel unduly charged with the survival of the family. They often cloak themselves in a premature mantle of responsibility, taking on some of the roles previously filled by the ill parent, such as cooking meals or caring for younger brothers and sisters. It is less threatening for them, at times, to assume these superficial aspects of adulthood than to come to terms with the frightening parts of childhood.

Other children may actively deny that there is anything wrong at all and become impatient or even rude toward the person who is ill. They behave as if the illness were an imposition and the world should revolve around their needs. This type of response usually draws a predictably different reaction from parents from that toward the apparently mature child who takes on extra responsibilities. Yet it may hide the same problems. It is a throwback to the magical thinking of earlier years. If children pretend there is nothing wrong, parents' illnesses may disappear. Even if they do not, at least the children can predict their parents' reactions. It is often more comforting to be able to predict even a hostile reaction than face the unpredictability of a parent's illness. Better the devil you know than the devil you don't, the child may reason.

In addition to fearing disease, children often have distorted images of medical treatment that cause a great deal of anxiety. Hospitals, especially, can be mysterious and terrifying places. Preschoolers are very concerned with body integrity, the reason why they may be concerned about what happens to their hair and their nails when they are cut. Their veneer of sophistication, gained, most often, through television, can belie some profound and important misunderstandings that frequently go uncorrected. One five-year-old child described his parent's upcoming operation as "It's like being in a fight. They cut you with knives."

Young children may become obsessed with matters that parents pay little attention to, such as what the doctors do with a tumor they remove. With their limited vocabularies they may force-fit new medical terms into more familiar words and, consequently, make false and frightening assumptions about illnesses and treatments. A four-year-old boy in Boston diagnosed with sickle-cell anemia told his psychologist that he had "sick-as-hell anemia."

Adolescents, especially those who anticipate leaving home soon, often react to parents' illnesses in ways that many adults find hard to understand. Although the teenagers may give the appearance of coping beautifully with the added stress in their lives, they frequently lie awake at night, wondering about the effect of their parents' illnesses on their transition to independence. They feel pulled toward their families and, at the same time, resentful of the constraints that having ill parents puts on the expanding boundaries of their lives. They feel embarrassed by parents who are different from those of their friends and then feel ashamed of their embarrassment. More than anything else, they feel alone.

Helping a Child Cope with a Parent's Illness

There will always be three questions in the child's mind, although they may go unspoken:

- "Did I make this happen?"
- "Is it going to happen to me or someone else I care about?"
- "Who will take care of me?"

The key to alleviating children's fears about ill parents is to give them the information they want in ways that they can understand. Unfortunately that is not as simple as it sounds. Children are often afraid to ask questions, for they've received a message, often unconsciously sent by their parents, that this is a topic to be avoided. Yet children's fantasies about illness are often much worse than reality.

One way to correct these misunderstandings is to have the child explain to you what is happening. Ask the child something like "If you were going to go home and tell your sister about this, what would you say?"

Certain things are, of course, beyond the ken of very young children. Even preschoolers, however, have a relatively sophisticated (although often inaccurate) concept of illness and death and will want information about what is going on when a parent becomes ill. Children will, through their actions more than their words, tell you how much information they can handle about a parent's illness.

Children who, in the middle of a discussion about something as stressful as this, start fidgeting or abruptly change the topic of conversation are not being rude. They are expressing, in the best way they can, that they have heard enough for now and need some time to absorb it all. Similarly, they may ask you questions that you know you've answered before. It is their way of getting comfortable with the subject.

Such behaviors will tell you whether you're being too open with your children about what's going on. They are built-in safety valves that children use to protect themselves from being overwhelmed emotionally. By looking for these types of responses, you can tell whether it makes sense to talk further, show your scars, or otherwise communicate with your children about what is happening and how it will and will not affect them.

Illness often means that parents become isolated from their children, allowing children to fear and imagine the worst. To help break down that isolation and to give your children tacit permission to ask questions, have them participate in some appropriate form of care for the sick parent, even if it's only bringing a glass of water. Those acts of caring help them feel involved and not excluded. They don't feel that important and mysterious family secrets are being kept from them.

If you are undergoing outpatient treatments, such as chemotherapy or radiotherapy, talk with your physician about having your children individually accompany you to a treatment session. The realities of such treatments are almost always much less frightening than the images of them conjured up by children. If that's the case, then attending a treatment session may lower children's anxiety about what's happening to their parents. Trust your instincts and knowledge of your children as to whether this would help them.

It may be useful to bring home photographs of the treatment room and any of the equipment that's involved. Photographs are also very good for preparing children who will be visiting someone in the hospital who is hooked up to tubes and monitors. Discussing the equipment and the noises ahead of time makes their strangeness less frightening.

In most cases, a nurse will stand with the children during the treatment to explain what is happening and to answer their questions. Those questions, however, are usually less important than the opportunity to see what is being done to you and observe how frightening or painful it really is. Although you should offer children who are mature enough the opportunity to watch such treatments, the decision whether to attend should be left up to the child. In some families with several children, a child may initially decline until he has heard reports back from his older brothers or sisters.

Maintain as much predictability in your children's lives as you can, so they do not feel that everything in their world is changing. Predictability brings about feelings of security for all of us. Simple routines, such as consistent meal times or watching a particular television program regularly, can help children feel more in control.

If you've had an operation, show your children the scars once they've healed. If you've lost your hair because of radiotherapy or chemotherapy, let them see what you look like without it. Some children who suddenly see their parent in a wig will assume that the parent's head has been left open or is deformed. Letting your children see you bald relieves that anxiety and lets them know that underneath all the signs of the illness, you're still you.

Finally, reassure your children that it's all right to enjoy themselves while you're sick. This is a terribly confusing time for many children, especially since they are told to behave differently when they are around someone who is ill and may be scolded for noisy behaviors that previously went unnoticed. Some adolescents appear to be especially affected by this belief that they should be somber around parents who are ill. It is a reflection of their growing but incomplete skills at empathy. They feel that if they are having fun when a parent is sick, they are somehow being disloyal.

Children's Perceptions of Death

We think of childhood as a beginning, a time with a future. To pair it with death is anathema. Few combinations of words make us as uncomfortable as "children" and "death." And so we all try, in one way or another, to protect our children from death and to preserve their innocence. There are times, however, when death intrudes upon the lives of our children. Most parents intuitively handle these situations very well, for their love of their children permeates the bad news their children must face.

Studies of grieving children conducted at the Judge Baker Children's Center in Boston and at other child guidance centers have found that the children who recover the best from the death of a parent or friend have accomplished four tasks:

• They have tried to understand the nature of death and why this particular one occurred.

• They have searched for ways to grieve for the dead person. There are many forms of grief, each suited to a particular child and situation. There is no "right" way for a child to grieve.

• They have searched for ways to commemorate that person. That commemoration may be literal, such as a memorial, or figurative, such as insisting on having Thanksgiving dinner exactly the way Mom used to have it when she was alive.

• They have tested ways to go on with their lives and to grow despite their grief.

A child's success at coping with those four tasks will be based, in part, on how you introduce him to death. By understanding the ways in which children at different ages comprehend and deal with the death of someone they love, you can help ease their fears and reduce their confusion. Although it was long presumed that children cannot comprehend death until they are about three years old, there is recent evidence that many toddlers appear to have some understanding of what it means. The sophistication with which children of all ages approach their understanding of death is a reflection of the major developmental issues they are facing, especially their ability to cope with abstractions.

It makes sense for your first conversation with your children about death to take place while they are still preschoolers. The cue for that first discussion may be your children's questions about someone who has died or a time when you pass by a cemetery or funeral procession. If no such natural opportunity appears, you should raise the issue rather than assume that your children have all the information they need. As with discussions about sex with children this young, you need not go into great detail. The implied message that you are open to talking about the subject may be as important as any specific facts you give your children.

If this conversation is triggered by the death of someone whom the children know and are fond of, it is best to tell them as soon as possible and to hold the discussion in familiar and comfortable surroundings, preferably at home. Holding your children's hands or embracing them when you talk about the death will help reassure them that they are not being abandoned. Trying to hide a death or postpone talking about it is almost always futile and may cause children undue anxiety since they cannot account for the stress among the adults around them.

Remember that many toddlers and preschoolers have difficulty distinguishing between hearing "bad" information and the "badness" of the message bearer. They may verbally or physically lash out at a person who tells them that someone or something they love has died or been hurt. This is usually not a sign that anything is wrong with the children. It is simply a normal reflection of their developmental stage.

Organizations that specialize in helping children handle death, such as the Good Grief Program in Boston, have found that young children have the least amount of trouble when parents use very simple and concrete terms, such as describing death as what happens when the body stops working. You can add spiritual or religious overlays to that description, although they may be beyond the comprehension of children that young. Remember that to toddlers and preschoolers, saying, "Grandma went to heaven," sounds just like "Grandma went to Peoria." They have no reason not to assume that she will soon return and that you'll pick her up at the airport. They wonder why everyone who was so excited and happy the last time Grandma went on a trip is now crying because she went on this one.

You can expect preschoolers and even older children to ask questions that are occasionally shocking. Will the dead person be cold or afraid of the dark? How will he breathe and go to the bathroom? When will he come out? Will he still need his wheelchair or his cane? Such questions, even after you've described death to children, are neither malicious nor rude. They are messages that the concept of death is too complex for them to fathom for the moment. They are also cues to remember and respond to their unasked questions about their own safety and status within the family.

A Preschooler's View of Death

When I was four years old, I asked my mother what happens when a person dies. She took that opportunity to give me an involved philosophical, humanistic explanation. My mother talked about how when a body is buried, it gives nutrients back to the earth. That helps the grass to grow. Cows eat that grass, she continued, and it helps them provide milk that is drunk by other children throughout the world. It was a very poetic description of the continuity of life.

Apparently it did not satisfy my curiosity, since I later asked my best friend from down the block, another four-year-old who was growing up in a devout Italian Catholic family. He told me about heaven and angels and clouds.

After listening to this, I marched back to my mother and announced, "Mommy, when you die, *you* can be eaten by a cow. I'm going to become a Catholic and go to heaven!"

Language can be a particular problem in describing death, because of both its abstract nature and the large number of euphemisms and colloquial expressions we tend to use. Children are least confused when parents use the word "death" rather than such words as "expire" or "lost." To young children, library books, milk cartons, and parking meters expire, each resulting in a different response. If you tell them that Aunt Gladys just lost Uncle Harry, they will wonder why she isn't out looking for him. If they become "lost," will their parents bother to look for them? Saying that a dead person is resting or sleeping peacefully or that a pet has been "put to sleep" may make naps and nighttime very threatening to children who are no longer scared of the dark. Similarly, some young children who are told that they are going to see a dead relative at a wake become very frightened. They are unfamiliar with the new term and think that they are being told they are going to see their dead relative awake.

Other expressions, such as "The good die young" or "God took away Grandpa because He loved him so much," may be very confusing and even scary to children. Does this mean that adults who keep telling them to be good really want them to die? If God loves them, will He snatch them away during the night?

Children's perceptions of death change dramatically as they grow older. By the time children reach early elementary school they often envision death as an evil spirit that comes to get people, especially if they can't run fast enough to escape. The image is similar to a game of tag in which death is "It" and chases after everyone who plays. By picturing death this way, children can imagine themselves immortal if only they can stay out of that fearful grasp. While this image makes sense when they hear about the death of someone who is old or very sick, children this age are much more confused when someone who is young and healthy dies. To resolve that conflict, they may call the dead person names or denigrate him or her in some other way, a response that frequently embarrasses and upsets parents. Realize that by doing so, children are creating a distance between themselves and their frightening image of death. Had it been they instead of the person who died, they strongly wish to believe, they could have run fast enough.

Adolescents may have a particularly difficult time handling death. They now have the intellectual abilities to understand that death is permanent and that we all are mortal. While they can no longer retreat into the dependent role of a younger child, they do not yet have the independence of an adult. They look around them for clues to what they should do and how they should feel. They often feel more comfortable grieving with their peers than with adults. Sometimes, however, they may view the death of someone in their family as embarrassing and try to hide it from outsiders.

There is no "proper" way to grieve. Although children's understanding of death follows a predictable pattern that is related to age, it would be foolish to predict that two school-age children or two teenagers will grieve in the same way. For some, the response will be immediate and tearful. Others may show little emotion because they need time for the realization to set in, because they did not feel close to the person who died, or because their style of grieving does not include the signs of distress many people assume to be normal.

Psychologists are just beginning to shatter the myths about grief and to recognize how wide a range of grieving is both normal and healthy. Recent studies of adults, conducted at the University of Michigan and the University of California at Los Angeles, found that many people do not have the expected period of intense distress and depression following the death of someone close to them. These people did no worse psychologically than people who were openly depressed and distraught. While some people worked through their grief relatively quickly, others grieved for several years. The differences appear to be simply a matter of personal style.

The third task children must accomplish following the death of someone close to them is commemorating the person who died. Trading stories with friends and family members about that person may help children realize that their memories are still warm and intact. Displaying mementos of the person may be a way of celebrating their relationship. These mementos need not be physical objects. A child may insist that a certain meal be served in a particular way because that meal is associated with the person who died. Roast turkey may not taste right without mashed potatoes and gravy because that's the way Grandma always used to serve it. That ritual, like other rituals around death, provides reassurance of the continuity of life.

The task of commemorating is especially important and often overlooked if the person who died was your child's classmate. When a young child dies, his teachers often clean out his desk while none of the other students are around. This adds to the mystery surrounding death and the feeling that it's something the children shouldn't talk about. Instead, teachers or parents should ask the children what they would like to do with the dead child's desk. Many children will want the desk put in a special place for a few months while they sort out their feelings. Some high schools hold memorial services for students who die from illness or accidents but ignore those who commit suicide. They are concerned that calling attention to a teenage suicide may glamorize it and possibly lead to more teenage suicides. Unfortunately, ignoring suicides tells children that we value some lives but not others.

All children need to participate in a ritual that acknowledges the death of someone close. For some that may be a ceremony at home; for others it may mean viewing the body or attending the funeral. It's best to give your children a choice of whether or not to attend the funeral. Never force a child to go. Ask your children what they expect to happen at the funeral, so that you can correct their misconceptions. If you bring young children to a funeral home, do it before or after regular viewing hours so that neither you nor your children are distracted by other visitors. If you bring young children to the funeral of someone close to you, have another adult come with you and take care of the children. They may become overwhelmed by the crowd or by the emotional intensity or simply not have the patience to sit still for more than a few minutes. The other person can take them outside or for a drink of water if the need arises.

Children and the Language of Funerals

Both parents had prepared their five-year-old son for the death of his seriously ill grandfather. They had spoken openly and answered the boy's questions about illness and death. Yet when the grandfather died, the young boy's behavior changed dramatically. The child grew pale and appeared terrified at the mention of a funeral. The parents, who were very concerned, brought him to a psychologist who had previously helped the child.

When he entered the psychologist's office, the boy burst into tears and screamed that no one could force him to go to the funeral. "I don't want to see Poppy with his head cut off!" he shouted. During their talk the child mentioned that someone had told him that when a person dies his body is put in a casket. Since five-year-olds are very literal in their thinking and since to a child that age the body starts at the neck, the only way the boy could envision someone's doing that would be by cutting off his grandfather's head.

Once the parents knew why the boy was scared and they could promise him that that wouldn't happen, he was able to go to the funeral and say good-bye to his grandfather. If he hadn't gone, he might have maintained for several years the fantasy that his grandfather was mutilated. If he had been forced to go, he would have been too terrified to look at the casket.

Finally, children must learn to go on with their lives. Sometimes children need help understanding how this is different from forgetting the person who died. It is as if their grief were the only thread by which they were hanging on to the person who has died. The distinction between normal and distorted grief is not in its form but in its intensity. While it may be beneficial for a child to deny for a short time that a dead friend or relative will never come back, continued denial is an obvious sign that something is wrong. Less obvious indications of a problem, however, are persisting feelings of anger, apathy, or guilt. Similarly, long periods of frenzied activity or continuing physical complaints, such as stomachaches or headaches, may be warning signs of unresolved emotional difficulties stemming from mourning. Working through such distorted grief usually requires professional help.

CHAPTER 13

Money

Understanding money is one of the most confusing, difficult, and emotion-laden tasks children face. Even as adults we carry with us strong impressions of our own parents' attitudes toward money. For many it was a subject seldom discussed with children. Money was as mysterious as sex, as steeped in ritual as religion, and as volatile as politics.

It is also a topic of continuing communication and miscommunication between parents and children. "How will they spend their allowances?" "Why can't we buy that new bicycle?" "If David's parents are taking him to Australia, why don't we go, too?" "What types of after-school or summer jobs make the most sense?" "May I have my own credit card?" "Which colleges may I apply to?"

Learning to communicate with children about an issue as symbolic, sensitive, and powerful as money requires that parents understand how children's stages of development influence their understanding of this sophisticated topic. Giving children appropriate financial responsibilities and experiences will help them tremendously as they enter adolescence and adulthood.

Why Money Confuses Children

The proliferation of credit cards, cash machines, and electronic fund transfers has made it more difficult for this generation of children to understand money than it was for their parents or grandparents. As personal finance has grown more complex, the misconceptions of children, especially teenagers, about money have become more insidious. That's why it's extremely important to teach children about the power and responsibilities that go along with money.

The task begins by knowing which concepts children of different ages have the most difficulty understanding. Misconceptions about money start early. A preschooler will tell you that nickels are worth more than dimes because they are larger and that five pennies that are spread out on a table are worth more than six that are stacked on top of each other. Paper money is valued less highly than coins. Even the slang terms we use to describe finances are confusing to a young child. When I was four years old, I spent a day at work with my father. That evening I told my mother that the people were nice, but I was upset because I hadn't seen where my father "made" the money.

By the time children reach kindergarten or first grade they understand that money can buy things. But the intimate connections between work and money or cash and checks are still unclear. Credit cards—which depend on the complex idea that money that is kept in a different place is going to be given to the store at a later time and that a few weeks after your purchase you'll pay a company that did not sell you the item you bought—are terribly confusing for children. Compounding this confusion are their observations that not only do you give the clerk the same card whether the item sells for ten or one hundred dollars but that you're given the card back with no apparent changes made to it after every transaction, unlike checks.

Parents usually use an allowance as their primary tool for teaching children about money. It's appropriate for children to begin receiving allowances as soon as they begin to realize that money can be exchanged for goods and services—usually when they're about five years old. The allowance should be enough for the child to buy something with it, be it a pack of baseball cards, a candy bar, a small toy, or a comic book.

One financial adviser I spoke with was confused by how differently his two children treated money when they were five years old. Each child received three dollars per week—considerably more than the national average of fifty cents per week in the 1980's. Every week his daughter put one dollar in her savings account and spent the other two dollars on books she wanted. His son, on the other hand, apparently felt an immediate need to divest himself of his assets as quickly as possible, especially if he passed by a video game. The boy's behavior is the more typical of a child that age.

The Purpose of an Allowance

Nearly every child gets an allowance starting around kindergarten or first grade. For many families it is little more than a ritual passed on from generation to generation. Yet receiving an allowance is a significant and symbolic step for children. It allows them to enter a world that is distinctly adult. It gives them a feeling of power and equality they may never have known before. Store clerks will sell them packs of gum without asking if their older brothers would also like one. Buying a comic book becomes a much simpler process when children don't have to ask an adult for permission.

Although most parents who give their children allowances also require that the children do some work around the home, such as taking out the garbage or clearing the dinner table, most child psychologists agree that it's a bad idea to link these two. As they grow older, children should be doing increasingly complex chores at home simply because they are members of the family.

Tying an allowance to specific tasks can backfire. It allows children to buy their way out of their basic responsibilities. If a child is supposed to clean his room or vacuum the house each week as part of his regular chores, and he decides he has enough money saved up, he may abdicate his responsibilities as a family member. The lesson he has learned is that all work is done for money.

On the other hand, it's sometimes appropriate for children to be allowed to earn extra money by taking on extra chores if they've done their basic work around the house. This helps young children see the relationship between work and money without thinking that they should be paid for everything they do at home.

Although parents should not control how children spend their allowances, you should be very clear about what you expect them to pay for and what other financial responsibilities they are assuming. These expectations will obviously change as they grow older and become more experienced at handling money. It's a good idea with older children to outline these responsibilities in a simple written contract (ideally written by the children and signed by both children and parents). The contract should include the parents' obligations as well as the children's. That way all know what's expected of them.

Do the children's allowances include lunch money? If so, what happens during school vacations? What will you do if they lose the money? May it be spent on candy and comic books? If they are teenagers, do they have to buy their own clothes with it? Can they borrow from you against future allowances? If so, how much and at what rate of interest or other penalty? How can they earn extra money? Will you ever hold back an allowance as a punishment? If so, under what conditions? When will the contract be revised? May it be changed before then?

Don't worry about using legal language in the document—although some adolescents may like doing it that way. Just be sure that all the children are clear about what's expected of them and what happens if they don't meet those expectations.

Talk to your children about the purchases they want to make. Help them think through the consequences of their purchases, but unless what they want is unsafe, allow them to make mistakes. If you insist that they make the "right" decision all the time, they won't get the most powerful benefit of allowances: the chance to learn more about themselves.

Even the most sophisticated parents sometimes have unrealistic expectations when it comes to their children's abilities to manage money. Young children have a very different awareness of time from adults. Next Tuesday is far into the future. Next summer is unfathomable. Saving money for college, when you're five or even ten years old, makes no sense at all. The dollar a week that the financial adviser's daughter put aside probably had less to do with the concept of saving for the future than with the attention her parents paid to her when she did it.

When you begin talking about saving money to a six- or seven-year-old, look for an item that the child wants to buy that costs more than one but less than two week's allowance. This is about as far as a child can delay gratification. Plan the purchase as a family. Go over the arithmetic together. It's important that the child understands that money today plus money in the future can buy something more than either amount alone. If the child doesn't want to go along with the idea, wait a few months. He's telling you that his mind isn't developed enough to understand the concepts involved.

By the time children are fourteen or fifteen their ability to plan for the future is usually in place. Children this age are ready to start receiving the allowances on a biweekly or monthly basis—pay periods that require more astute financial planning if the money is to last.

Remember that the money you give your children to spend is exactly that: money they decide how to spend. Although it's always appropriate for parents to set constraints on what their children will buy, such as not allowing certain toys or such dangerous items as firecrackers, the basic choice of how to spend the money should be left to the children. Children who occasionally or even frequently squander their allowances may, in fact, have an advantage over those who spend it all on parent-suggested items. One value of allowances is to permit children to make relatively small mistakes in a controlled situation. You can do less financial damage dribbling away your allowance at age eleven than making the same mistakes with credit cards a decade later.

Parents who respond to wastefulness by cutting back on a child's allowance or taking financial control may be doing more harm than good. Parents who consistently give children all the money they ask for are probably doing a similar disservice. Learning that money spent on a hamburger will not be available for a movie—and that Mom and Dad will not always give you the extra money for that movie—is an object lesson in life as an adult. So is learning that buying something you want does not always bring happiness—or learning that giving some of your money away to a charity instead of keeping it all can help you feel good.

Financial Training Beyond Allowances

There are a few things in addition to paying allowances that parents can do to help young children become more financially sophisticated.

Try to take the mystery out of money. Talk openly about the aspects of family finances that children can comprehend. For school-age children that may be allowing them to practice their arithmetic by figuring out which can of vegetables costs less per ounce or researching which days and times movie theaters have reduced-price shows. One job that will allow a teenager to learn about living expenses is to have him prepare the checks (for a parent to sign) that pay the family's routine bills. By participating in family meetings to discuss major purchases or vacation expenditures, teenagers learn how buying one thing often means being unable to afford something else. Be sure to let children know what financial information should be talked about only within the family.

A particularly creative approach was taken by one family whose children didn't understand why their parents couldn't get them everything they wanted. The more the parents said no, the more demanding the children became. One day the parents cashed their monthly paychecks, brought the cash home with them in dollar bills, and stacked it on the dining-room table. The children were clearly impressed and excited by how large the stack of money was.

The parents gathered the whole family around the table, where the children helped divide the money into piles, each representing a bill that was due or a projected expense, such as food for the upcoming month. When they were through, the children saw how little was left on the table for discretionary spending. They stopped asking for as many things.

Teenagers and Jobs

Aside from allowances, the most common way adolescents obtain money is through part-time jobs. Yet the notion that holding down an after-school or weekend job helps build a teenager's character and eases the transition into adulthood may be based more in the folklore of Hollywood than the realities of the 1990's. Several recent studies indicate that for many adolescents, holding typical after-school jobs may do just the opposite by distorting the teenagers' perceptions of adult work and of economics. Whether your child will benefit from part-time employment depends on your family's finances, the number of hours the child works, the type of job, and how he spends his earnings.

When Frank Capra begins his classic film *It's a Wonderful Life,* he shows us a teenage George Bailey working after school at the town drugstore. George's job requires a lot of responsibility and independence. His diligence even saves the life of a customer and salvages the reputation (and the business) of his employer. Each week George hands his paycheck over to his parents to help them send his younger brother and him to college. Through this job he learns new skills, practices handling adult responsibilities, and contributes to his family and his future.

This mythical situation is a far cry from today's typical after-school job scooping up fries at the local fast-food joint. Nor is holding such a job while an adolescent likely to help a child in nonfinancial ways. Surveys of high school students conducted by the Institute for Social Research at the University of Michigan since 1975 have shown that for most children holding typical teenage jobs, the stress of working while attending school took a serious toll. These researchers found that the more hours a high school senior worked, the more likely that child was to use cigarettes, alcohol, and illicit drugs to help cope with the added stress. Those children who worked more than fifteen to twenty hours per week had the most problems.

The ideal part-time job for a teenager offers three types of experiences:

• It helps the child develop knowledge, skills, or attitudes that will help him as an adult worker.

• It helps him work with adults in such a way that he feels a part of the adult world.

• It allows him to contribute meaningfully to the financial success of his family or community.

Yet many teenage jobs offer none of these experiences. The work, especially in fast-food restaurants, is often mindless, unskilled, and repetitive. Instead of breaking down a barrier between generations by having them work together, the typical teenager's job isolates him with other teenagers.

What the jobs do offer is money—usually the minimum wage for fifteen or more hours of work per week during the school year. Yet according to a study by the National Center for Education Statistics, children living in poverty had the lowest rate of after-school employment. The highest employment rate was among high school seniors in families whose incomes, in 1980, were greater than twenty-five thousand dollars per year. The greatest demand for teenage workers is in the suburbs; the lowest is in the inner city.

The way most teenagers spend the money they earn at part-time jobs leads to another problem. The surveys made by the Institute for Social Research found that fewer than 10 percent of seniors who worked contributed at least half their paychecks toward family living expenses. Fewer than 13 percent saved half their earnings for their education. More than 60 percent spent most of their money on clothing, entertainment, and eating out.

What this does, unfortunately, is teach children a distorted sense of values, for they learn that the major portion of a paycheck is for discretionary spending. That distortion can get children into trouble when they no longer can rely on their parents for food, clothing, and shelter.

For families that do not need their children's wages for survival, the most beneficial after-school work is at volunteer jobs. Unlike the typical minimum-wage work most teenagers land, many volunteer jobs meet all three of the ideal job criteria listed earlier. The jobs may be challenging and complex. The teenage volunteers are more likely to work with adults, apply skills they have learned in school, and receive specialized training. They also may better see the benefit of their work.

The roots of these differences are easy to see. The only motivation for working at a fast-food restaurant is financial. The employer has very little incentive to make the job interesting or provide additional training since a newly hired employee can do the job well within a few hours. Replacing a worker who quits is relatively simple.

Volunteers, however, work for other reasons. The employer must make the job challenging and enjoyable instead of counting on a paycheck as a motivator. Also, volunteer programs have a vested interest in building up the skills of a worker by providing additional training and experiences. Replacing a volunteer is not as simple as replacing a minimum-wage worker.

One national study in 1982 compared high school students who did volunteer work with students who did paid work and those who had no outside jobs. Student volunteers showed larger gains in their ability to solve problems, were more reliable, had greater growth in their self-concepts, and received more valuable information about adult work.

Also, having done volunteer work may give teenagers a long-term financial advantage as well. The skills learned by volunteering at a nursing home or community center are usually perceived by employers as more valuable than experience wrapping hamburgers.

Financial Problems

Financial troubles are the most private of problems. They bring forth emotions we wish we did not feel. They can split a family apart or inspire a stronger relationship. To many parents, telling their children about financial problems is nearly as upsetting as the job loss, divorce, bad investment, or whatever else that led to the situation. Our reluctance to discuss money problems may come from a sense of pride, a desire to protect our children from bad news, or fear of being embarrassed by having that news spread throughout our community.

There is no simple answer to the question of how much information about financial problems you should share with your children. When parents get their children overinvolved, the children often think, "My family's falling apart, and I've got to do something about it." Although these impulses spring from good intentions, the children do not realize how unrealistic and inappropriate they are. And so we hear stories like those about a seven-year-old boy whose father lost his job and had no savings. The boy did break dancing during school recess to collect coins from other children to give to his father to buy food. While the intentions were good, the costs were great, for the child felt an overwhelming responsibility that he could not meet and the father felt that his son's handful of coins was yet another sign of his own inadequacy.

The opposite extreme—trying to hide everything from children—is often fruitless and may do more harm than good. We pretend that things are OK and try to protect our children from the financial pressures we are feeling. But in most cases the facade is not persuasive and may cause far more problems than the truth. An accountant friend of mine has a client who lost his job as a sales executive four years ago and has been earning far less as an independent sales representative. The man will not explain the extent of his financial crisis to his teenage daughter, who is used to spending freely, because he does not want to upset her. The daughter knows something is wrong, but she will not ask questions for fear of distressing her father. She continues to spend. He keeps on borrowing. Each is worried and alone.

Children are emotional sponges. They can feel the tension in the family, even when it's covert. Trying to hide such a problem from a school-age child or a teenager often causes the child to imagine the circumstances to be far worse than they really are. Children may also interpret your combined evasiveness and discomfort as a sign that they are somehow responsible for causing the bad situation. Many parents, when they speak to their children several years after a stressful event, are surprised by how much information the children actually knew at the time. Sometimes the parents are also surprised by how much of that information was incorrect.

The ways children learn that something bad has happened to a parent also influences how they interpret what is happening. Children who learn upsetting information by overhearing it tend to exaggerate its importance. Those who hear it directly from their parents will look to those parents for cues to how to respond and how upset to become. They quickly try to determine if their parents are still stable enough to provide them with the security they need. The younger the child, the more he needs to know that the family's financial problems and the parents' moodiness aren't his fault.

Family financial problems may have positive effects, however. For some children, especially adolescents, seeing a parent fail not only may show them how to cope with a similar situation but may also substantially improve their relationships with their parents. Paradoxically, the parents who benefit the most are often the ones who think they need it the least. In general, the more competent the parent, the greater the benefit to the child of the parent's admitting the problem. Children of very competent parents often fail to see their parents' vulnerabilities. They find their parents' constant apparent success intimidating. Perfect parents are unapproachable parents. Hearing those parents admit that they, too, have problems makes these children feel closer to them.

Telling Children About Money Troubles

Children's responses to their parents' feelings and statements usually have more to do with their stages of development than with the parents' situations. To a four-year-old, money is only vaguely connected with his or her own simple form of demand-side microeconomics. Two small cookies are always better than one large cookie because there are two of them. One cookie now is always better than two cookies later because the child doesn't understand the concept of later. Giving children this young financial details will only make them upset.

Children under the age of seven will often interpret a parent's offhand comments literally. Figures of speech like "We may lose the house" may conjure up terrifying images of the child's bedroom walls being torn apart while the child is in her room. Children in late elementary school or junior high school may feel equally overwhelmed, but they handle the pressure differently, often becoming angry and striking out.

Even a sixteen-year-old who is earning money at an after-school job may find some economic problems confusing and a bit frightening. Those fears may be well founded, for financial trouble is often a part of a larger tear in the fabric of a family. Children may ask questions like "Why does the divorce mean we have to sell the house?"; "What does the stock market plunge have to do with which college I can attend?"; "Does Mom losing her job mean that we'll have to move away?"

Begin by addressing the child's unspoken fears:

- "Am I safe?"
- "Will I be abandoned?"

Telling your children, for example, that although you've lost your job, they're not going to lose you will prevent unnecessary worries and open the way for effective discussions. It's very reassuring to children to hear you talking about the steps the family will take to remedy the situation. Let them know why you may be canceling a vacation or that you are trying to stretch the food budget by buying less lamb and more chicken. Ask the children to suggest ways they could help meet the family's goals.

Even small children may make contributions and should be shown and told that these count. Young children may share toys rather than ask for new ones. They, as well as older children, may limit their demands for new clothes or other items. Teenagers will often offer to get part-time jobs so that they can pitch in. Yet the image of a teenager directly contributing to the rent check leaves many parents uncomfortable. Perhaps more disquieting is the offer of a six-year-old to sell lemonade or his toys so that he, too, can help. As sincere and unrealistic as that offer is and as genuinely helpful as a teenager's offer can be, they may be very upsetting to a parent who interprets them as signs of failure.

Although a teenager's offer to contribute some money to the food budget might be considered, let your children know that money is not the only way to help out. Emotional support to help everyone weather the rough times can be more highly valued than dollars.

CHAPTER 14

Puberty

The Hurdles of Puberty

The growth of children into adolescence puts parents' skills at communicating with them to the test. To many parents, the thought of their children going through puberty raises feelings ranging from ambivalence to dread. They fear that the physical changes of adolescence are a sign that their relationships with their children are going to change as well. Parents expect the surge of hormones that leads to new body hair, changing shapes, and cracking voices also to bring about dramatic changes in their children's behaviors, including increased moodiness, defiance, and outbursts of anger.

At the same time adolescents must learn some new and critical skills from the adults around them. Yet their behaviors toward those adults, especially their parents, may be confusing and apparently counterproductive. That confusion bespeaks what the children are going through as they follow their paths to independence and adulthood. Adolescence is marked by battles over power and control. It is a time of physiological stress as children cope with what seems like a conquering army of hormones. It's also a time of emotional stress as they try to adjust to the new demands made on them by family, peers, and school. The combination can test the mettle of even the most sophisticated parents.

But recent research at Pennsylvania State University and elsewhere indicates that the physical changes of puberty are not directly responsible for the common changes in adolescents' behaviors and that the Sturm und Drang are not as common as many parents believe. Those studies are also challenging myths about the timing of puberty—myths that have caused concern for parents and children alike.

Around the turn of the century psychologists and psychiatrists assumed that the normal hormonal changes of adolescence caused all children to engage in violent emotional upheavals and bitter battles with their parents. Although some battles—such as the ones over power within their family—are to be expected, many children make the transition from child to adult with a relatively low amount of emotional turmoil and only a healthful amount of confusion and rebelliousness. Yet surveys of parents and teachers continue to show that they tend to have stereotyped views of adolescence and expect the changes to be much more extreme than they actually are.

One possible reason for the increased arguing and tension is that our culture does not have a clear rite of passage that quickly defines the beginning of adulthood. Getting a driver's license, with all of the power and freedom that it implies, is the closest thing to a symbol of maturity. Instead of providing a marker for entry into adulthood, we spend the years between when our children reach sexual maturity and when they live independently giving them mixed messages about their roles and status. We tell them they are important, but we do not let them vote or enter into contracts. We sell them cosmetics and clothes by convincing them that they must be sexy, but we also tell them that they cannot be sexual.

Moodiness and Maturity

Teenagers usually respond to the stress in their lives with a combination of regression and emotional growth. It is a time of wide fluctuations in mood, when even a minor criticism can trigger a very dramatic response. One day your twelve-year-old is behaving like a sophisticated young woman; the next day she's as demanding and dependent as a nine-year-old. For some adolescents, there is even a recurrence of anxiety-related problems they suffered as young children, such as nail-biting, teeth grinding, and bed-wetting.

The mood swings and testiness often lead to family arguments and rebellion at school. One critical battle, however, occurs at home. Adolescents want more of a say in decisions that affect them and their families, yet they may not know how to express that adult need in an adult manner. Rather than express their feelings directly—indeed, they may not be able to express these new feelings to themselves directly—they choose an extreme example that challenges their parents' authority and their own status as children.

Consequently, a fourteen-year-old girl may ask if she can come home at 2:00 A.M. on a school night or mention that she'd like to borrow a razor because she admires another girl's shaved head. Many parents, for whom the idea of their child's shaving her head or staying out most of the night are among their greatest fears, react by doing exactly the opposite of what the teenager is trying to accomplish by those poorly chosen requests: They try to wrest more control away from the teenager. They take away her privileges and limit her independence. The resulting fight is predictable.

Such battles over extremes may often be avoided by involving children in growing numbers of important family decisions as they get older. This involvement also gives your children a safe place to make mistakes and a chance to practice, under your gentle supervision, thinking through the types of problems they will soon face as adults. How should they plan their time? How must they weigh the consequences of their decisions and actions? By being allowed to participate more fully in family decisions, ranging from what to eat for dinner to how to budget money, adolescents do not have to prove their independence and maturity by rebelling in the same ways as children who are locked out of this entry to adult responsibilities.

This does not mean, of course, that you should accept an inappropriate or dangerous decision simply because your children want to do it. Allowing a young teenager to stay out until 2:00 A.M. on a school night (and just about any other night, actually) is both unsafe and unwise. The consequences could be dramatic and irreparable. It is not an appropriate or beneficial way for the child to express independence and should simply not be permitted. While parents may disagree with the aesthetic taste of a fourteen-year-old girl who wants to shave half her head, the odds are that the new haircut by itself would cause little, if any, long-term damage. The hair can always grow back. It is a relatively risk-free way to rebel. (Also, rebelling isn't as much fun if your parents don't put up a big fuss.)

Teenagers and Telephones

To understand how teenagers communicate with their parents, it's useful to take a closer look at how they communicate with one another. Adolescents have a natural affinity for telephones. This device, which was largely ignored during the earlier phases of childhood, is now treated as if it were a natural appendage of their bodies, an electronic extension of their mouths and ears. There is good reason for this newfound attraction, for there is much more to teenage telephone use than what parents often perceive as idle jabbering.

One recent study of telephone use found that girls in the fifth and sixth grades averaged 30 minutes per week on the telephone. Boys that age averaged 15 minutes per week. By the time they reached ninth grade, girls were spending 180 minutes per week and boys were spending 50 minutes per week on the phone. Also, teenagers use telephones differently from both younger children and adults. While an adult may use the telephone to call a stranger or someone he or she has not seen for a long time, teenagers often feel awkward and uncomfortable with such conversations. Instead, they use the telephone to talk with the very people they've been with all day. Parents often find this confusing. Why would a fourteen-year-old girl, for example, come home from a school dance and immediately call her friends (who all had been to the same dance) to recount in great detail what had happened less than an hour earlier?

The answer is reflected in the developmental issues teenagers are facing throughout puberty. They are constantly trying to discover who they are, who they should be, and how they compare with others. Although Alexander Graham Bell never intended it for this purpose, the telephone is an ideal tool for tackling such questions, for it provides intimacy as well as a certain amount of anonymity. The teenager who calls up her friends immediately after a dance is asking, in effect, "Did you see this event the way I saw it? Are my perceptions accurate? Am I interpreting the world in the same way as my friends?"

Part of the increase in telephone use by teenagers parallels a general increase in the amount of time adolescents spend in all types of talking. Younger children spend much of their time outside school playing and little time sitting down and speaking to each other. By the time they reach adolescence, that pattern of activities begins to change. They feel a much greater need to talk with someone their own age who's going through the same experiences. They also have a much greater ability to talk about abstract issues. Those new and more sophisticated thinking skills make talking much more interesting and attractive.

The telephone's unique combination of intimacy and privacy allows adolescents to test their new skills and new areas of adult behavior without risking as much embarrassment as they would in person. They don't have to be as conscious of their facial expressions and their gestures as they do in person. That can make the telephone a powerful and very helpful tool for teenagers who are shy. The boy who feels too uncomfortable to talk to a particular girl in the school hallway for fear of looking foolish or otherwise embarrassing himself in public may feel less exposed and vulnerable on the telephone. That is why many teenagers use it as a way to ease themselves into dating.

There are several guidelines to help parents handle their adolescents' increasing use of the telephone:

• Help teenagers understand that telephone use is a privilege, not a right. It's sometimes very effective to make telephone use contingent upon certain behaviors, such as passing courses at school and finishing chores at home.

• Set limits on lengths of calls and hours for telephone use, but make sure they're realistic. Teenagers often benefit greatly from conversations that parents sometimes see as trivial. Although it may be expedient to get your children their own telephone line—especially if you have several teenagers—there are also advantages to sharing the line with them since they must learn to cooperate with the rest of the family.

• If you arrange for a separate telephone line for your children, set up clear rules for its use. Many parents find that their children's friends quickly learn to call the parents' phone number if the children's line is busy, leading to a resurrection of the problem that made the family pay for the extra line in the first place.

• Set up a system for paying the telephone bill, especially long-distance charges. Will your children have to pay for all their long-distance calls or only for those that aren't made to relatives? Will they be able to use the telephone on "credit" from you? What happens if they can't pay their contribution when it's due? Having partial responsibility for a monthly telephone bill is an excellent way to ease teenagers into the autonomy they'll need when they leave home.

The Timing of Puberty

Although both children and parents worry about the effects of being a very early or very late bloomer, studies at Pennsylvania State University have shown that contrary to popular belief, passing through puberty earlier or later than their peers has little lasting effect on most children. One notable exception is girls who reach menarche (their first menstrual period) between the ages of nine and eleven, approximately two to four years earlier than the average girl. Menarche usually follows most of the other physical changes associated with puberty in girls.

These early-developing girls appear to be at a higher risk for a poor self-image throughout high school. The physical changes they undergo in grade school often make them feel as though they no longer fit in with their classmates. They feel fat and uncomfortable with the changes in their bodies. Many of the girls who mature early respond by trying to socialize with older girls. This leads to new discomforts and more feelings of awkwardness and not belonging, for they aren't mature enough to handle the typical behaviors of the older group. Their bodies have outpaced their other stages of development. They can't think in more mature ways. They're not more sophisticated simply because their bodies have developed. They seldom have the self-esteem and social skills they need to handle the pressures they may feel from the older girls.

The few studies of boys indicate that for them the timing of puberty appears to have little lasting effect. Early-maturing boys, in dramatic contrast with early-maturing girls, usually say that they're quite pleased that they're becoming bigger and stronger. Late-developing boys may have some temporary problems with self-esteem, but that is quickly remedied once they have caught up with their peers. In fact, late-blooming boys may be trading a temporary discomfort for a lasting advantage. According to one study by Dr. Anne C. Petersen at Penn State, by twelfth grade late-maturing boys have higher self-images than other boys.

Puberty is a time for many types of growth. It's difficult to associate the gangly young man who's already two inches taller than you, or the attractive young woman who's meeting her new boyfriend at the movies, with the baby you protected from all harm only a few years earlier.

Parents may be confused and even frightened by their children's behavior as they go through the physical and emotional changes of puberty. Usually the physical changes outpace the emotional ones, often causing parents and teachers to have unrealistic expectations for these children. They see the developed bodies and falsely assume that there has been equivalent emotional and intellectual growth. Yet emotional, intellectual, and physical growth during puberty is distinctly uneven. This unevenness may be especially frustrating to parents, as when teenagers' growing abilities to reason are matched with their newly developed but very imperfect skills at questioning other people's statements and challenging their authority. The adolescents' pride in their increased ability to think logically comes across, instead, as arrogance and intolerance.

Another sign of that uneven growth is often teenagers' acute emotional sensitivity about the physical changes they are undergoing. Few families celebrate the onset of these physical changes. The secretiveness with which we treat them tells children that we are ambivalent about their new bodies and changing identities. One study of pubescent girls done by Dr. Jeanne Brooks-Gunn, a developmental psychologist at the Educational Testing Service in Princeton, New Jersey, found that two thirds of them said that they had been teased about their breasts, with many saying that it was their parents who had done the teasing. Yet many of those parents were apparently unaware that their mundane comments about the changes their daughters were going through were being perceived as teasing.

Talking About Sexual Issues

Although every generation secretly prides itself on being the first to discover sex (an illusion that makes moonlight liaisons all the more romantic), there is little that today's adolescents do in the way of sexual behavior that their great-great-grandparents did not do. The control of unwanted pregnancies and of sexually transmitted diseases is, from the standpoint of technology alone, quite simple. Extremely effective contraceptives have been available for years. The spread of AIDS and other sexually transmitted diseases can be either stopped or dramatically diminished by the use of condoms.

Unfortunately children, especially adolescents, often act in ways that appear to defy logic. Sometimes the reason is basic: The teenager has not been given the facts about sexuality and the sexual transmission of disease. That may be because of the parents' discomfort over talking about sex or their beliefs about what a child should and should not know at a given age. Among parents who think they've been open about sexuality and whose children are acting inappropriately, the information about sex may have been presented in a way that was difficult for the child to understand and to feel free to question. Usually that's not a matter of the parents' or teachers' using too complex a vocabulary, but of their failing to take into account how children and adolescents at different stages think and how they express themselves.

No matter how open parents have been in dealing with sexual issues throughout their child's development, adolescence marks a change in the tone of those discussions, for it's a time when sexuality and sexual activity cease being theoretical. The time when children need the most information is also, many parents believe, the time when they are least receptive to getting that information from their parents. But those children are listening more closely than they let on. To assume they are not is to do them a great disservice.

Talking to an adolescent about sex is often an anxiety-provoking experience. The specter of AIDS frightens parents, especially since teenagers tend to have three characteristics that put them at great risk: Their sexual activity is often impulsive, they feel that they're invulnerable, and they have difficulty planning ahead. These characteristics combine to contribute to the relatively high rate of teenage pregnancy despite the increased availability of contraception. Many parents fear (without basis, I think) that simply talking about sexual intercourse will be interpreted by the child as tacit permission to be sexually active.

Parents and teachers who came of age during the sexual revolution of the 1960's and 1970's find themselves counseling a more conservative and cautious approach to sex than they perhaps took as adolescents. At the same time they worry that their newfound conservatism may form a barrier between the generations. After all, as adolescents they rallied to the cry "Don't trust anyone over thirty!"

What these parents forget is that the last thing in the world adolescents can afford to do is let their parents know that they value their parents' opinions. There's good reason for this. Adolescence is a time for testing new forms of independence. These emotional and intellectual steps toward adulthood are awkward and wobbly, but unlike the first steps of a toddler, they often occur in a context of fear and isolation. "The other kids look like they have everything under control. I must be the only one who's having trouble. If I admit I'm having problems, then the people I care about (my family and my friends) will think less of me. Therefore, I'd better keep it to myself and look like I know it all already."

The adolescent's reluctance to appear awkward or unknowledgeable is often compounded by the timing of discussions of sexuality. All too often these talks between teenagers and their parents are triggered by negative and emotionally charged events, as when a classmate becomes pregnant or a rape occurs in the neighborhood.

Adolescents often find the thought of rape or pregnancy extremely unnerving. Yet because they worry about rejection or ridicule if they admit their fears, they feign nonchalance. Their peers do the same thing. Each walks around encased in a thin bubble of bravado, believing "The others are strong, and I am the only one who is weak." And so they listen intently and just as intently try to give the impression of not listening.

Another event that usually triggers a talk about sexuality occurs when a teenager first falls in love. Parents often feel anxious about this and, depending upon their own adolescent experiences, may try to protect their children from emotional disappointments. Children are likely to perceive this protective attitude as meddlesome rather than caring. By labeling their experience "puppy love" and by telling them that they'll get over it, we give children the message that we think that their relationships are inconsequential and that we don't take what they are doing and feeling seriously.

Yet a first love may be the most intense and overwhelming love a person ever feels. It occurs, not coincidentally, at a time when adolescents are trying to sort out and understand the subtleties of emotions. As if that weren't enough to cope with, two other factors enter into play. The physical and hormonal changes the child is undergoing are obvious and usually acknowledged by parents. Often forgotten or misunderstood, however, is that one of the tasks of adolescence is separation from parents.

Separating from family is pretty scary stuff, especially since teenagers tend to approach most things in life as all-or-nothing propositions. Falling head over heels in love is one way to test that separation. It allows the child to experiment with independence without giving up the feeling of belonging.

It is no wonder that children bristle when we belittle their first experience with adult love. They are dealing with much more than a crush or infatuation. It is a flirtation with adulthood.

When you understand that, the moodiness and emotional sensitivity of an enamored teenager make much more sense. The person an adolescent falls in love with is as much an emotional safety net as a paramour. Denying the importance of that safety net instills panic and anger. It also makes the teenager cling more tightly to it. A first love may not be mature love, as adults understand it, but it is both strong and extremely important.

Talking to Your Teenager About Sex

All this theory about the effects of adolescent development on their perceptions of sexuality is of little use unless you can find a way to put it into practice when talking to your own children about sex. Here are some guidelines for talking to teenagers that can help establish open communication and ease some of the tensions around sexuality.

First, recognize what you can and cannot control. You cannot control your child's sexuality. After all, your parents couldn't control yours. If you try to take control, your child will simply rebel, and with good reason. You can—in fact, you will whether you want to or not—*influence* your child's sexuality. The effectiveness of your influence is related to your skills at communicating. To communicate well, you must understand the context in which your children are growing up. What are their personalities like? What are they capable of understanding at both intellectual and emotional levels? What are the pressures they are feeling and supports they are receiving from their friends, family, teachers, and others who are important to them?

Make intimacy of all types, including sexual intimacy, a regular topic of discussion rather than a special subject. What makes friends different from strangers? What does "love" mean? Ideally these talks should start when a child is in preschool and should continue after a child becomes sexually active. That doesn't mean that it's too late to start if your child is already a teenager. It's just that your task of making sexual feelings and activities easily and openly discussed topics may be harder than if you'd started a decade earlier.

Don't talk about love and sex as isolated topics. Instead, help your children to see them within a context of emotions. How does love feel different from jealousy? How does sex relate to sharing and openness?

If you feel anxious talking about sex, admit those feelings to your child. First of all, you're not fooling anyone if you pretend you're not uncomfortable. A child who is nervous about asking questions or expressing new emotions will be looking at least as much at how you say things as at what you say. Unless you acknowledge the discomfort or conflict, your emotions rather than your words will convey your message.

Also, your anxiety may actually work to your children's advantage. If you admit that you're uncomfortable, it makes it easier for your children to acknowledge their discomfort. You're showing them an alternative to keeping their embarrassing or otherwise upsetting feelings to themselves. You're also allowing them to choose between accepting and rejecting your emotions. Children who accept your uneasiness are likely to believe that you will reciprocate by accepting their uncomfortable feelings.

In the same vein, share your own experiences with dating and being in love for the first time. How nervous were you? What did you do? What pressures did you feel? Dig deeply into your memories, trying not to overlook the awkwardness and embarrassment of your own adolescence.

A good working rule is that anyone can ask any question

but that no one is obligated to answer if he or she believes the information is private. Some of your thoughts and behaviors are none of your children's business. Some of their thoughts and behaviors are none of yours. Not sharing everything you do with your parents is a part of growing up. Insisting on knowing everything from your children is denying their maturation.

Let your children know what your values are. Adolescents in particular need a set of standards to compare with the values they are starting to try on for size. If you believe, for example, that your children should not engage in premarital sexual intercourse, you should share not only that belief but also the reasons behind it. That will help your children see your moral or religious beliefs as more than just arbitrary rules. Attempting to accommodate your children by being "modern" may actually be doing them a disservice. The task of grappling with and evaluating (often confused with rebelling against) values is a critically important step in preparing to lead an independent life.

Finally, show your children that you will not reject them if they make a mistake. This gets to the core of an adolescent's anxiety about independence. Even if you strongly believe that your children should not have sexual intercourse before they're married, it's important that they have information about appropriate and effective contraception and protection from sexually transmitted disease. While you're telling them your values about sex at their age, you're also telling them that you value their lives more. It's like saying to your children that you don't want them to drink alcohol before they're adults but that if they do drink, they shouldn't get behind the wheel of a car.

Remember, you cannot control their sexual activity any more than you can control their physical growth. Trying to do so is worse than a waste of time; it is building a barrier between you. It ignores the critically important context of their sexuality while focusing on the content of their sexual activity.

CHAPTER 15

Entering Adulthood

Learning to Be an Adult

The picture of adult life we paint for our children is filled with false colors. We lower our voices so they cannot hear us discuss the bankruptcy or the love affair. We wait until they're asleep before we air our frustrations and anxieties. Shielding our children from things that might upset them is part of the parent's job. We view childhood as a carefree time of life, without the stresses and problems that surround us as adults. Through our children we, too, can be carefree—if only vicariously.

The desire to protect our children runs counter to the need to prepare them for independence. While helping children ease their way through that transition, parents face a series of important decisions that slowly chip away at the innocence of their children and, the parents hope, replace it with a stronger mortar. How much should we shield our children from the adult world? Should we share everything with our children? Are our sex lives any of our children's business? What about our family's finances? At what age is a child able to understand "adult" information?

The ways in which we communicate about adult topics with our children, and the timing of that information, are critical to their developing the skills they need to have independent lives. The things we say and do provide more than just information. They provide permission for our children to try out aspects of adult freedom and responsibility in a safe environment, where the cost of failure is minimal and the rewards of success are recognized by both parent and child.

Knowing what to share with our children, and when to do so, can help them grow into confident, competent adults. To do so requires understanding how our children think and looking for clues to their emotional and intellectual development. Some information is simply beyond the ken of young children. Three-year-olds, for example, cannot understand abstract concepts. If a child that age cannot see it or touch it now, it may as well not exist. Telling your three-year-old the reasons for your divorce or the problems with your investments is simply a waste of time. The complexity of emotions may even be beyond what a thirteen-year-old can handle.

But even your children's chronological ages are not very good predictors of what they can understand. You must look at their psychological or emotional ages as well. One way to tell what your children can handle is to look at the papers they write for school. How close to adult thinking is the logic of those papers? How do they deal with emotional issues?

Children will also let you know how much they understand by the types of questions they ask. For example, few children younger than ten understand the relationships among work, income, and life-style. While they may sense the distress in their family, the concept of Daddy's being out of work means very little to them. They will want to be reassured that the stable parts of their lives—parents at home, food on the table—will not be disrupted. A teenager, however, has begun to see the relationship between a job and money and will ask questions about the job market and salaries. In either case, your answers should be tailored to the level of your child's question. If your child leaves the room or becomes inappropriately angry or upset, it's probably because the child still doesn't understand the information and is frightened by it.

Although our intentions may be good, some of the ways we try to protect our children may be causing as many problems as we are trying to prevent. Let's take the situation where two parents are having a loud argument. Their four-year-old son overhears the commotion and walks into the room. The father, concerned that if the child sees his two parents fighting he may think they'll split up and abandon him, tries to protect his son. He tells the boy he wasn't really angry. He was just kidding.

While well meant, this type of dishonesty may have several bad effects, especially if it occurs regularly. Most children see the lies for what they are. They know what anger sounds like and wonder how this could be something else. What could be so terrible that their parents would try to hide it from them? Instead of feeling more secure, they may develop a general distrust of what their parents say.

What better way for a child of any age to learn how to deal constructively with anger and frustration than to see those behaviors modeled by his parents? A child who sees strong emotions that are openly acknowledged is less likely to misinterpret those emotions than one whose parents try to cover things up. By admitting that you're angry or frustrated or sad, you are providing a context for your child to understand what you're doing and what you're saying. Perhaps more important, you are showing your child that it's OK for him to express emotions, too. As a parent you don't have to be perfect in the way you handle your own anger in front of your child. If you occasionally show how upset you are, your child will learn that regardless of what he often sees on television, adult anger need not lead to violence.

What about sex? How much should your children know of your sexual interests and activities? While psychologists are divided on exactly what you should share with your children, there are some guidelines. You do have a right to your privacy, just as your children have a right to theirs. What you share with your children, and how you share it, should go no farther than your level of comfort.

Remember that what you say should match the child's level

of comprehension and emotional maturity. A preschooler, for example, not only would not understand sexual activity but might even find it frightening. While it's probably not in the best interest of young children to see sexual intercourse, it's not as traumatic as some psychoanalysts describe, and all is not lost if this happens. Once again, the types of questions your child asks will tell you whether he or she is upset or simply curious.

Keep in mind that children learn at least as much from context as they do from content; your children will learn and remember more from how you present things than from what you say. If you are upset and uncomfortable discussing sexual issues with your children, they will feel uncomfortable discussing their own sexuality. It's extremely important, however, that your children recognize from a very young age that their parents are sexual beings. All children should see their parents hugging, touching, and kissing, for these are the precursors to a child's learning about intimacy.

Trying on Adulthood for Size

Making the jump from child to adult is no simple task. Late adolescence is marked by vacillations between self-assurance and dependency. It's a bit like learning to walk, as teenagers take tentative steps into adulthood while still holding on to their parents for support. It's an ambivalent grip, for the adolescents at once clutch at the security of the past while desperately resenting the urge to do so. Parents, too, feel torn. Having a child leave home marks the end of an era within a family. It is a time both of celebration and of mourning.

Preparing a child for independence is, perhaps, the ultimate goal of a parent. It is a process that begins soon after birth. The first tasks are matters of practicality and convenience. We teach our children to feed and dress themselves and how to use the toilet. Beyond that first stage of independence, both parents and children are often uncertain. Although we want to send our children to school, we're a little disappointed if, on their first day, they abandon us without shedding a tear. A child may respond to the responsibilities of living with a new baby by "forgetting" how to control his bladder. In both cases we are torn between the excitement of our changing status and the comfort of our old relationships.

The key to fostering independence is to provide a structured environment in which children may make mistakes without hurting themselves. For example, although you should choose the food, a child in elementary school should learn how to make a simple lunch. The amount of peanut butter or tuna fish the child puts on his bread is of little consequence compared with the feeling of accomplishment making that lunch brings.

Perhaps more important than any physical skills are practice and comfort with making decisions. A preschool child should be offered clear alternatives: "Would you like to have the book or the doll?" A grade school child should be able to handle more complex choices and should begin dealing with contingencies: "If I keep saving my money for the bicycle, I won't be able to buy the baseball bat for two more months." By the time children reach adolescence, they should feel comfortable determining whether they need more information before making decisions, and should know how to find that information.

Allow your children to make mistakes. People learn best by experiencing the natural consequences of their behavior. A child who teases a cat will quickly learn and always remember how a cat expresses its displeasure. More important, the child will learn that one scratch does not mean the relationship with that cat is doomed. You can recover from mistakes.

Encouraging independence does not mean abdicating your responsibilities as a parent. Your six-year-old may be able to choose what shirt he wears, but he should not have the option of playing in the snow without gloves. He's too young to understand the danger of frostbite. By the time he feels pain in his hands, he may have seriously hurt himself.

Similarly, your teenage daughter's decision to date should be made within the moral and social guidelines you provide. Apparently arbitrary rules made by parents cry out to be broken by children. Involving your daughter in developing rules that fit within your guidelines gives her a greater sense of control over her life. Breaking such a rule is no longer simply a way of showing anger with her parents.

Although the fostering of independence begins with infants, it accelerates during the teenage years. The family provides the safest and most forgiving environment in which an adolescent can test the skills of adulthood. Parents who discourage their teenagers' autonomy by denying them the opportunities to make mistakes and trying to correct them are making the transition to adulthood more difficult for these children. Cooking all of your teenagers' meals, arranging for their jobs, and taking care of all their money are not kindnesses, even if the children appreciate the help at the time.

Psychologists at college and university counseling services have repeatedly told me of their surprise at the number of eighteen- and nineteen-year-olds who are not prepared to live away from their families. Many freshmen feel uncomfortable making the simplest decisions on their own, for they have not had enough opportunity to practice the fundamental skills of adulthood. Some quickly become overwhelmed and drop out of school. For others, their temporary solution to the problem is to abuse alcohol or other drugs.

Such problems are by no means limited to college students. Filling out a first employment application form at age eighteen can be frightening. Not balancing your checkbook because you don't understand how is courting disaster.

But what if your child is already sixteen or seventeen and is still very dependent? He may need some remedial work to catch up with other children his own age. That work may have to start with basic cooking and financial skills. It's easier to practice these skills if they're introduced one at a time. The consequences of mismanaging an allowance or part-time wages while living at home are less serious than getting into debt while living away from home for the first time.

The benefits of such practical, remedial work extend far beyond knowing how to make a meat loaf and balance a checkbook. The confidence gained from such successes will help adolescents feel better about themselves as people. Knowing that you can do something as basic as sewing on a button or fixing a broken toilet can make the thought of living away from home seem a lot less daunting.

Some adolescents who've mastered the basic practical skills of independent living still lack confidence in their abilities to survive on their own or at college. Several approaches may help them feel less intimidated. Talk to them about their past successes with adult responsibilities, such as working at an after-school or weekend job. Encourage them to spend a weekend away from home or to care for the house while you spend a weekend away. A more powerful (and delightfully sneaky) way to help them build their self-confidence is to ask them to teach a few of the independent living skills to a younger child. Teaching will give timid adolescents a sense of mastery of the subject and an awareness that they are truly different from younger children.

The Move to College

To college-bound high school seniors, April 15 has nothing to do with taxes. College admissions offices send out the majority of their acceptance and rejection letters during the first two weeks of April. To an applicant, the daily trip to the mailbox is often filled with both dread and anticipation. For most students, the fear is that they will be rejected. For a few, it is that they will be accepted and will no longer be able to retreat into the dependency of childhood.

While all high school seniors, including those planning to attend local colleges or junior colleges and those directly entering the work force or the military, are acutely aware of the changes they must soon face, those applying to colleges far away from home are struggling with a different and often more intense pressure. It is often felt the most by those students who are trying hardest to please their parents by getting into the "right" schools. During the fall and winter of senior year, when they were filling out applications, gathering transcripts, and writing essays, their active involvement gave them a feeling of control over the college admissions process. As April 15 approaches, they must abdicate that sense of control while they simply wait to hear the results of the judgment. Such passivity does not sit well with most students who are motivated and talented enough to apply to college.

That process of applying to college is in many ways symbolic of the transitions teenagers face as they enter adulthood. Choosing where to live and how to spend your time is adult behavior, as is coping with financial aid.

According to some psychologists, the so-called senior slump, in which some students cease being involved with their academic work and extracurricular activities once they've been accepted by colleges, is simply a way of safely easing into that transition. The emotional separation from school becomes practice for the upcoming separation from their parents. Students who, for the first time, fail a course during their senior year of high school may be having a lot of difficulty with that separation. Suddenly failing a course may be a way of holding on to some of the security of childhood.

Acceptance and Rejection

Although deciding which college to attend isn't the most important decision your children will ever make, it may very well be the most important and stressful decision they've made so far. While college rejection letters may leave a student feeling depressed and frightened, so may acceptance letters. Students who get into the colleges of their choice often find themselves wondering if they made the right choice to begin with. Here are some things you can do to make the most of the process of college selection:

• Try to keep things in perspective. Even those students who have received only rejection notices can apply to schools that take late applications or can spend a year doing something else and then go through the cycle again the next year. This is a time when children need unqualified support rather than criticism. Children will be listening for even the slightest hint from their parents that they are failures. This is a time to rally around them.

• Don't think of a school's rejection letter as a comment on the value of your child as a person. It's simply its admittedly imperfect estimate of how well an applicant met its many needs. Help your child make this distinction as well. Often high school seniors will blow college rejections out of proportion. Occasionally parents do the same. Give your child a break. Don't talk about what might have happened if the child had studied harder.

• If it's financially feasible, students should consider making second trips to the colleges before accepting the schools' offer. Seeing campus life from the perspective of an accepted applicant will often make some of their jitters disappear.

Orientation to an Independent Life

A mother I interviewed joked self-consciously about whether her college-bound son would be able to get up in the morning to go to class. "I've been his alarm clock for I won't tell you how long," she told me. "He assures me that whenever he's been away, he's done it. I have no way of knowing whether it's true, but I guess I trust him."

For parents about to see their children leave home for college, such practical and extremely common concerns signal a recognition that something extraordinary is happening. Freshman year at college is often an adolescent's first taste of sustained independence. But the equally important challenge for parents is less talked about. The first year at college leads to struggles not only with the changes in their children but with their own identities and their perception of the nature of a family.

Since their children were born, parents have referred to them as "my child," "my son," "my daughter" with hardly a second thought about the implications of those possessive terms. Now that has changed, as the bonds of possession become less physical and more emotional. We can hear the stress during parent orientation programs at colleges. Throughout most of the programs the entering freshmen and parents attend separate presentations and workshops. As the reality of the upcoming separation hits home, the most common question asked of the administrators is: "When will I see my kid again?"

Parents' concerns are compounded by the dramatic changes colleges have undergone since the days when they were in school. Students are treated more like responsible adults. Colleges no longer view their role as *in loco parentis*. Freshman courses are seldom prescribed by the schools. Social rules, such as dormitory visiting hours and curfews, have almost all been abolished. The bulletin boards are plastered with notices for bulimia support groups and AIDS awareness workshops, emphasizing the abrupt shift from the more cloistered setting of home.

Even the most sophisticated and calm parents can have trouble providing just the right mixture of encouragement and support for their departing children. After all, how do you say, "Good-bye, but we're with you"?

Easing the Emotions of Freshman Year

While having some sort of difficulty during the first year at college is common enough to be considered a rite of passage, there are some things parents of freshmen can do to help their children through this transition to adulthood and independent living:

• Recognize that students want control over when they call home. They don't mind doing it regularly, but many of them don't want parents to call them.

• Regular mail from home, especially when it includes clippings from the local newspaper and the occasional care package of goodies, may be very helpful to students trying to adjust to their new school. A few homemade cookies or a picture from home may help ease the stress of writing a term paper.

• If your child calls to say she hates her roommate or the food is awful, don't rush in to help. The best thing you can do is let her vent her feelings without passing judgment on what she's saying. If, when she's through talking, she still feels the same way, encourage her to solve the problem herself by going to the resources on campus.

Returning Home as an Adult

A woman in Chicago told me about her college freshman son's first visit home from school. "He started calling his dormitory home," she exclaimed. "And if *that* doesn't wound you as a parent . . ."

For most college freshmen, their first trip home occurs over the Thanksgiving holiday. In many families it marks the beginning of a new level of relationships between parents and children. It takes awhile for those new relationships to sort themselves out. When the child walks through the door, the parents see what looks like the child who left them a few weeks earlier. But he has begun to think of the campus as home and to carve out a life for himself away from his family and old friends.

Those feelings of independence are ambivalent and are punctuated with a combination of rebelliousness and regression that many parents find confusing. The returning children bristle when their parents ask what time they'll be home at night and seek out opportunities to enlighten family members on politics and economics. Friday night is spent discussing the strategic lessons to be learned from the Peloponnesian War. Yet on Saturday morning they may spend hours staring at cartoons on television.

They may revel in their newfound independence, insisting on retaining the social freedoms they enjoy at school. Their lives have changed. They are now adults. But if their old bedrooms—that most tangible link to their childhood—have been converted to other uses or, worse yet, given to younger siblings, they are outraged. It is easier to risk an advance when you know you have the option of retreating.

Understanding the cause of these mixed messages begins by recognizing that for many children the first few weeks of college are as terrifying as they are exhilarating. At the same time these students are acutely aware of the efforts their parents have made to send them to college. They come home shell-shocked from their first round of serious academic challenges, especially if they are bright students who were able to coast along during high school. During this first visit home they feel compelled to show their parents that they're working and struggling. Complaining about how much work they have to do, how far behind they are, how bad the food is—all this is a way of communicating to their parents that they have risen to the occasion and that Mom and Dad are getting their money's worth.

They have also changed in subtle ways they're not aware of, as they soon discover when they seek out high school friends to compare notes on college life. After the opening banter, in which each talks about how much harder he or she has it than the others, the spirited conversation often deteriorates into an awkward silence. They feel estranged from their high school friends, for they no longer share so much in common. The awkwardness is a form of mourning, for they have lost something that was a large part of their lives and must move on to new levels of relationships.

Parents, too, are learning new roles. Much more of their children's lives are now hidden from them. They pump their children for information about their new friends, their courses, their exams. The responses are often halfhearted or absent, for those are the last things college students want to be quizzed on at this time. Most important is receiving the reassurance that their places in their families have remained intact.

Celebrating the Changes in Your Child

"Don't freak out!" advised a university dean I interviewed for advice on how parents should handle the changes in college students coming home for the first time.

Don't be overly concerned with college freshmen's complaints about the stresses of college life. Parents who have spent years helping their children overcome difficulties find it especially hard to listen to complaints without intervening. Instead, focus on the students' emotions rather than the ostensible content of the problems. Acknowledge the difficulty of the struggles. Simply allowing them to ventilate their emotions is often the best help you can offer.

Although your child's first visit home may appear pretty chaotic, it's a necessary disorganization. That visit is a time to let go of many of the symbols and roles your child grew up with. It's especially important to remember that underneath all the superficial changes your child is still the same person.

Freshman year of college is a time to shed the skin of childhood and test the limits of being an adult. Much of that testing comes through rebellion against their own past. Students often reject family traditions, such as attending church services. Staid conservative families are greeted by daughters who espouse Marxist doctrines. Parents who pride themselves on their left-wing politics cringe when their sons describe the social benefits of joining the Young Republicans Club. It's important that parents not retreat from what they believe. By disagreeing with your children on fundamental issues, you're reassuring them that there is a corner of stability in their lives and that you haven't changed your values on other, perhaps more important issues that they have not raised.

Remember that your children may be intoxicated by their newfound adult roles and may tend to argue naively about adult issues. This is a time for patience and tolerance, for the ideas and the ways they are expressed are less important than the attempt to tackle this aspect of adulthood. Your children are not yet fluent in adult discussions and, although they may appear arrogant, are likely to be especially sensitive about their awkwardness. The amount of time you spend listening, and the manner in which you do it, will answer their unspoken questions of your acceptance of their new status.

Most of all, your children need to know that you are still there if they need you but that you have confidence in their abilities to handle things on their own.

General Index

Age-Finder Index

Infants

Toddlers

Preschoolers

School-Age Children

Adolescents